Leadership the
Ozarks
Way

Robert L. Perry

ISBN: 978-1497566071

Published by Organizational Health Associates
P. O. Box 3, Willard, MO 65781
www.organizationalhealth.org

DEDICATION

I dedicate this book to my mother and father, my grandparents, my aunts and uncles and all of those Ozarkers who built lives on these rocky hills and wide prairies. They not only survived droughts, tornadoes, floods, snakebites, economic depressions and wars; they taught us how to live and how to overcome. They taught by their words, their engaging stories and by their examples. Whatever following generations of Ozarkers achieve, we all are deeply indebted to those who made straighter and clearer the paths for us.

ACKNOWLEDGMENTS

I acknowledge the outstanding men and women who were part of my survey group. They were very generous in sharing their time and the details of their lives with me. Each of these is worthy of a lengthy memoir to preserve his or her legacy of leadership. Until those memoirs are written, I hope this small tribute honors their hard work and deep faith. I have included an appendix in the book that provides a brief introduction of each person as I have come to know him or her.

I acknowledge my Ozarks family. When we returned to Missouri in 2003, it was with the hope that we would build strong and binding ties with our family in the area. That experience of being with family has exceeded our fondest expectations. We treasure, not only the family we have gained by birth, adoption and marriage, but the broader family of church and friendship.

Finally, I acknowledge my wonderful wife, Dr. Marilyn Nelson. Marilyn has been my companion, friend, partner and spouse for over 20 years. She is my best friend and my dearest love, second only to my devotion to God. Marilyn is a very skilled editor; she assisted me at every step of developing this book. She proofread every line, and made helpful suggestions and important corrections. I pronounce Marilyn to be an honorary Ozarker with all of the rights and privileges pertaining thereto.

Table of Contents

A brief summary of the author's background as a native Ozarker, an explanation of terminology used in the book, and an affirmation of the Ozarks culture as good preparation for life and leadership.

An overview of the area called "the Ozarks," and a short summary of its history.

A summary of the author's interviews of 20 persons from the Ozarks who achieved significant leadership roles in various fields and parts of the world. This includes the interview questions which were explored with each person and a brief summary of their responses.

Some history and personal anecdotes about how basic honesty is taught in Ozarks culture.

Ozarkers are taught to value family and to be loyal to those they consider family. In most cases they are blood relatives, but in some instances they apply to the larger clan with which one identifies.

A strong work ethic is endemic to Ozarks culture. The primarily rural background of many Ozarkers taught them to work hard and expect others to do the same.

Ozarkers learn to be innovative in the ways in which they address setbacks. When the tractor quits you fix it with what you have at hand.

When the cow has trouble giving birth you get your hands messy. Solve the problem the best way you can.

Preface

I grew up in the Ozarks. My boyhood included plowing the fields with a small Ford tractor, milking the cows morning and evening, putting up hay bales, weeding the garden, shoveling cow manure out of the barn, fishing in a farm pond and hunting squirrels in the woods that surrounded our house. Much of the time I disliked that way of life (except for the fishing and hunting). I did not like the hard work, the isolated living and the constant demands of tasks that never seemed to find an end. I longed for life in the "big city" with its constant movement, excitement and variety of things to do. I knew early on that life on the farm was not for me, and that education was "the way out." It was only in later years that I came to more fully appreciate the beauty of the Ozarks and the strengths of the culture.

The Ozarks Mountains of south Missouri and north Arkansas are not the rugged, snow-capped mountains you might see in the Rockies. They are large hills, often covered with dense vegetation – a mix of oak, ash, hickory, maple, pine, cedar and many other trees. The large hills form deep valleys that often hold spring-fed streams of clear, cold water.

The soil on our hilltop 80-acre farm was rocky and poor. Except for river bottoms, farming the land in our part of the Ozarks is the very definition of "hard scrabble." Thousands of small family farms dotted across the Ozarks provided only a minimal subsistence, and most of the farmers had to hold jobs "in town" to keep their families fed. Many of those small, family farms have disappeared.

The people of the Ozarks, my people, have often been dismissed as "hillbillies, rednecks, hayseeds, bubbas, white trash, trailer trash, etc." The broad stereotype is that Ozarkers are stupid, simple, ignorant and toothless. For many people outside the Ozarks, their impressions have been shaped by television shows such as the Beverly Hillbillies and Hee

Haw. Entertainers like Jeff Foxworthy and Larry the Cable Guy have built careers on the "hillbilly" persona.

The word "hillbilly" is thought to have first appeared in print in an article in the *New York Journal* referring to someone who lives in the hills, knows poverty, drinks whisky and carries a revolver. "From this point on journalists and travelers applied the term *hillbilly* to the marginal farmers of the southern mountains." [1]

Dr. Brooks Blevins, the Noel Boyd Professor of Ozarks Studies in the history department at Missouri State University, says that "hillbilly" is a landmine word. It is used among native Ozarkers as a self-deprecating way of referring to themselves, but it often has negative and derogatory connotations when used by those who are not native to the Ozarks. It is a bit like the forbidden words that have sometimes been used to refer to African-Americans. They may use those words within their own groups, but it is considered highly offensive when outsiders use them. Because of this, Dr. Blevins generally avoids the use of the word, and I shall do so as well in the rest of this book except when quoting others. [2]

Academics also generally prefer to use the term "Ozarkers" to refer to Ozarks natives as opposed to "Ozarkians." Outsiders to the area have sometimes used the term Ozarkians in a negative or derogatory way. [3] Once again, I will utilize the term Ozarkers in most instances unless I am quoting another author.

As I write this book, with the intention of celebrating the heritage shared by those of us who were fortunate enough to grow up in the Ozarks, I acknowledge the danger inherent in building exaggerated positive stereotypes. The prideful embrace of a positive stereotype can be as far from reality as the hateful embrace of a negative stereotype.

Brooks Blevins notes that there is an ongoing debate within academia about the issue of "regional exceptionalism." As we study the culture of various geographic regions, there is a temptation at times to exaggerate the value of a given cultural stereotype. Since it is generally considered inappropriate to judge racial, regional or other groups based on negative stereotypes, one must also be careful not to imply that a particular regional culture is necessarily superior to others. [4]

My concern in this book is not to engage in regional exceptionalism by saying or implying that the culture of the Ozarks is inherently superior to other regional cultures. However, I would like to note that the people of the Ozarks are generally honorable, honest, unpretentious, strong and good. The child of the Ozarks need not feel any lack of self esteem because of a rural upbringing, having attended a small school or lacking some of the advantages of her urban counterpart.

I suggest that the predominant culture of the Ozarks provides one with an excellent platform on which to build life and leadership. This platform for leadership is much more than the basic beliefs and values with which one is raised and which are taught by his or her parents. It goes back many generations – through multiple generations in the Ozarks, coming from the Appalachians, and earlier from Scotland, Ireland and England. Many of these core qualities passed through so many cycles of generational transmission that they are almost a part of the DNA of the Ozarker.

Foundations are important. The quality of the foundation determines the soundness and quality of whatever is built upon it. That simple truth is beautifully illustrated by Jesus in the parable with which he closes his Sermon on the Mount. In Matthew 7:24 and following Jesus talks about the wise man who builds a house on a foundation of rock, contrasted with the foolish man who built on shifting sand. When the storm came the house with a poor foundation fell; the house with a firm foundation stood.

That is how I have come to regard my heritage in the Ozarks. It provided for me a sound foundation. The values that were taught and the lessons that were learned became the basis on which I would make decisions, decide moral issues, exercise faith and generally direct my life. I attribute whatever success I have had in leadership roles as having been built on that foundation. Some of these transcendent values and qualities are strength of character, problem solving (learning on the farm to fix things with baling wire and binder twine), integrity, loyalty, hard work, resilience and faith.

Chapter One – The Ozarks: Its Geography and Culture

The Ozarks is a mountainous region that includes most of northern Arkansas and southern Missouri. It is a large section of the center of the United States that includes more than sixty thousand square miles.

The name Ozarks is thought to have come from the French words "bois aux arcs" (literally, "wood of the bow") referring to the wood from which the native American Indians made unusually strong bows. This wood was from the Osage orange tree, which also is called the bois d'arc tree. The term was eventually "shortened to Aux Arcs and anglicized to the present 'Ozarks.'" [5]

The Geography

As a geographical area, the Ozarks is frequently divided into smaller sub-regions based on variations in terrain and elevation. These sub-regions include three hilly or mountainous areas. These are:

1. The Boston Mountains that run through the southern portion of the Ozarks in Arkansas. These Mountains run east and west from a about 20 miles south of Fayetteville to about 20 miles south of Batesville.

2. The White River Hills that run southeast from about 20 miles west of Branson, MO to Batesville, AR.

3. The Osage Gasconade Hills that occupy a rough circle with about a 20 mile radius around Osage Beach, MO.

There are two less hilly areas of the Ozarks that are comprised of prairies and gently rolling hills.

1. The Springfield Plain which runs east and west and takes in most of the area between Joplin, MO and Springfield, MO.

2. The Central Plateau that runs southeast from north of Lebanon, MO to south of West Plains, MO. [6]

Early Inhabitants

The earliest known inhabitants of the Ozarks were Native American tribes that made their homes in these hills and valleys as early as 12,000 B. C. By 1,000 B. C. there is evidence that indigenous tribes developed pottery, began to use the bow and arrow for hunting and engaged in farming. By 1700 A. D., the major tribe in the area was the Osage, who claimed most of the Ozark Plateau by 1800. This included territory "from the Missouri River on the north to the Arkansas River on the south and the Mississippi River on the east to the western prairies." [7]

By the early 1700s Native Americans were joined by European explorers and settlers. "The earliest white settlers, for the most part itinerant trappers and fur traders, principally of French or French-Indian origins, apparently touched only lightly into the Ozarks, taking little and giving nothing except a rather widespread scattering of French names…" [8] Those French words are reflected in the names of towns (Bois D'Arc), rivers (Bonne Femme), and lakes (Pomme de Terre). Even the name of the region, "Ozarks" reflects the French influence. Serious settlement of the Ozarks by Caucasian immigrants expanded in the later 1700s. "Springfield, Missouri, the oldest of the present major Ozarks towns, was first incorporated during 1812." [9]

These early European settlers who established communities in the Ozarks in the 1700s came from the southern Appalachian mountains, predominantly from West Virginia, southwest Virginia, Tennessee and Kentucky. These were people of Scots-Irish heritage who immigrated to the Appalachians, stayed there briefly, then came to the Ozarks beginning in the 1750s. They came primarily because of the availability of land, and because the mountainous terrain was familiar to them. [10]

The Scots-Irish Immigration

This reference to Scots-Irish heritage raises another matter of terminology as to whether the proper term for the ancestry of many Ozarkers is "Scotch-Irish" or "Scots-Irish." It is generally thought that those who come from that heritage prefer "Scots-Irish." One old-timer observed, "**Scotch** is whiskey; the people are **Scots**." Thus, I will call them Scots-Irish except in direct quotes from other writers.

In his book, *Born Fighting*, Senator Jim Webb of Virginia does a masterful and scholarly job of tracing the roots of the Scots-Irish immigrants from their battles in Scotland, their departure from there to the Ulster Plantation area of Northern Ireland, and their immigration from Ireland in the middle 1700s to the Appalachian areas of the US. From there, many of the Scots/Irish migrated west to Kentucky, Tennessee, and eventually to the Ozarks of southern Missouri and northern Arkansas.

Many things about the rugged hills of the Ozarks appealed to these hardy people who suffered and fought for generations in Ireland and Scotland. Webb notes that descendants of Scottish ancestry scattered around the globe. "And wherever they traveled, they would bring with them an insistent independence, a willingness to fight on behalf of strong men who properly led them, and a stern populism that refused to bend a knee, or bow a head, to anyone but their God." [11]

Jim Webb also suggests that even though the Scots-Irish heritage includes only about 20% of the population of the United States, it has tended to be a dominant culture. "In these early years, at every step of the way, English, German, and other settlers inter-married and joined these communities, but the sheer numbers and cultural power of the Scots-Irish would shape and define the mores of America's rural heartland, particularly in the South." [12]

In his compelling autobiography, President Jimmy Carter notes the same cultural heritage that has been so influential in the American South and Midwest. "It seemed natural for white folks to cherish our Southern heritage and cling to our way of life, partially because the close ties among many of our local families went back another hundred years before the war, when our Scotch-Irish ancestors had come to Georgia from the British Isles or moved south and west, mostly from Virginia and the Carolinas." [13]

Many of us who are a part of this Scots-Irish cultural heritage have not been conscious of that part of our family history and failed to fully appreciate the strength and quality of the generations from which we descended. We tended to allow our sense of "belonging" to a culture to be defined by those relatives we have known or with whom we had personal experience.

Ozarks Heritage Contrasted with Other Agrarian Cultures

Many aspects of life in the Ozarks are not unique to the Ozarks. The philosophy of "agrarianism" describes the rural lifestyle as inherently superior to urban ways of life. In Wikipedia, M. Thomas Inge defines agrarianism as a belief that the cultivation of the soil produces a positive spiritual good. Direct contact with nature, he says, produces "honor, manliness, self-reliance, courage, integrity and hospitality." [14]

One might try to equate the agrarian culture of the Ozarks with other agrarian societies, but there are as many differences as there are similarities. One example of an agrarian lifestyle is found in the Amish communities in the United States. Comparing the Amish farm life to the Ozarks rural life, there is a difference in the level of requirements and disciplines expected of children and youth, as well as adults. The Amish are guided by a set of rules called the "Ordnung" which specifies how they dress, the length of their hair or beards, horse-drawn buggy styles, farming methods, and may other matters of daily life and conduct.

The Amish also have typically provided 8 years of private school education for their children with a strong element of religious education. In contrast, most Ozarks children attend public schools and are encouraged to complete high school and aspire to education beyond high school. The Amish practice a religiously-motivated separatism designed to keep them apart from the evil influences of the sinful world. Ozarks children, even though they may be nurtured in very religious families and communities, have not been subjected to that degree of separation from general society. [15]

Another possible culture of comparison to the Ozarks is the Scandinavian-influenced farm life common to the upper mid-west. These farm families in Wisconsin, Minnesota and that general area share much with Ozarkers. The strong work ethic and appreciation of cultivating the soil certainly are shared values. However, the culture would be different due to the strong influence of the Scots-Irish tradition in the Ozarks and the Scandinavian influence in the northern area.

The Scots-Irish predisposition for fighting is one difference. The Scandinavian heritage is likely to be more peaceful and peace-loving. There is a significant difference in the musical and storytelling heritage of these cultures. The styles and methods of farming also vary greatly because of the "hard-scrabble" efforts required of Ozarkers, dealing with rocks and poorer soil.

Various attempts have been made throughout the history of the United States to create "utopian" agrarian societies, such as the Oneida Community in New York state and the New Harmony community in Indiana. This was an experiment in communal living and the sharing of property, possessions, and even communal parenting of children. These agrarian societies were generally short-lived and are not very comparable to the long-term rural culture of the Ozarks.

The Ozarks Changing from the Farming Lifestyle to a More Urban Character

Recent decades brought about significant changes in the Ozarks. Historian Brooks Blevins notes that the Ozarks began to develop as a tourist destination in the early 1900s as a result of the publication of the book, *Shepherd of the Hills* by Harold Bell Wright. That book sold 2 million copies by 1918, and it spurred a tourism boom that continues to this day. The story deals with a distressed city pastor who retreats to the Ozarks to find peace and quiet to recover his emotional and spiritual strength. It is a story of redemption, love and renewal, and it presented most of the local Ozarks residents in a positive light. [16]

The development of Marvel Cave along with Shepherd of the Hills tourism, both near Branson, led to the growth of a major theme park, "Silver Dollar City." The popularity of country music shows in the Branson area led to famous and less-famous musicians coming to the area to make Branson a mecca of live music shows. The lakes in the area (Table Rock, Taneycomo, Bull Shoals) brought water sports and fishing as draws for visitors, retirees and part-time residents.

This development of tourism in the Ozarks has had a profound impact on the culture, and makes it very different from that experienced by Ozarkers prior to the modern era. By the middle of the 20th century, the modern world invaded the peace and quiet of the Ozarks. "The price of modernization, even in the most rural backcountry areas of the region, had been the demise of the local community and the loss of a traditional culture and way of life fashioned by frontier demands, isolation, and hardship." [17]

But even though life has changed for Ozarkers compared to what it was 50 years ago, the beautiful hills and prairies still hold a place in the hearts of our grandchildren and great-grandchildren. We still smell the springtime fragrance of fresh-mown hay. The neon overkill of the Branson strip does not have much in common with the moors of Scotland, but we still have the blood of the clans flowing through our veins. Those of us who grew up without indoor plumbing or electric lights are passing from the scene, but the character of our heritage will go on. The rest of this book will attempt to explore some of the elements of that character.

Chapter Two - Leadership Interviews

Research for this book included the reading of the books noted in the bibliography as well as other books and articles. In addition to reading, I felt that I needed to hear the stories of at least 20 persons who shared the common culture of either growing up in the Ozarks or adopting the Ozarks as their place of residence for a large portion of their lives.

That group of Ozarks leaders includes: Vernon Armitage, Ann Ashcraft, Hosea Bilyeu, Winston Burton, Nolan Carrier, Bob Dale, Thomas Field, Mike Haynes, Waylen Jobe, Arthur Mallory, Bob Marti, Russell Newport, Ryan Palmer, Patti Penny, Bill Rowe, Harlan Spurgeon, Paul Swadley, and Chuck Williams. I am deeply grateful to each of these, and several others not listed here, who shared their inspiring stories with me.

This group was chosen from my own acquaintance with persons who have been professional colleagues, personal friends and/or generous mentors. Each one is an Ozarks success story and an example of effective leadership in his/her area of enterprise. I was interested in the particular issue of leadership with concern for how the prevailing culture of the Ozarks enhanced the individual's leadership toolbox. I focused primarily on folks of my own generation (I was born in 1945), this generation being the last one that commonly grew up with an agrarian way of life. We knew the adventure of toilet needs being met in an outhouse, had a home heated with a wood stove, and were reared by parents who well knew the rigors of the Depression and World War II.

The average age of the research group was 70, with a range of ages from 40 to 92. The group includes ministers of high-profile mega-churches as well as bi-vocational ministers of small churches. There are eight doctoral degrees among the group, three university presidents, two NCAA Division 1 coaches. Several have been denominational executives. One of the group retired as an Army Brigadier General (one star). One of the group is an internationally-known tenor and recording artist who graduated from Harvard University and studied at the New England Conservatory of

Music. Two of these are business entrepreneurs who built and ran multi-million dollar enterprises. Two served as missionaries in overseas settings. Each one of these should write a personal memoir to preserve his or her life story, her lessons learned and his philosophy of leadership. Until those memoirs are published, perhaps this small volume will serve to remind us to appreciate our heritage, celebrate our ancestry and learn from one another's life experiences.

The common element for all of them is the Ozarks. Some stayed and led organizations in the Ozarks; others left the Ozarks and achieved success in far-flung places. Nearly all of them (all but two) chose to return to the Ozarks to work or to retire in these beautiful hills. Most of them grew up on farms located near Ozarks towns like Neosho, Buffalo, Chestnut Ridge, Verona, Bolivar, Joplin, Marionville, Lockwood, Stotts City and Seymour.

On the next pages I will share the list of questions that I discussed with those I interviewed. In most cases these questions served as conversation starters, and the interviews turned into shared recollections of home, family, church and community. Sweet nostalgia was part of the discussion, but it went much deeper than that as stories of pain endured, challenges faced, failures overcome and faith exercised came forward. These people are among my heroes, and I am proud to share their Ozarks heritage.

Questions for Ozarks Leaders Interviews – 2012

1. Where were your ancestors from? In Europe? In the US? How long in the Ozarks?

2. How do you feel about the Ozarks? Have you lived other places? How did that feel?

3. Growing up did you wear any "homemade" clothes?

4. How far did your family have to drive to get groceries?

5. Did you grow up rural or urban?

6. Do you know how to milk a cow? Butcher a hog? Castrate a calf? Drive a tractor/combine?

7. What smells remind you of childhood?

8. Did your earliest home have electricity? Indoor water? Indoor bathroom? Radio? TV?

9. What did your Dad do for a living? Your Mom?

10. How many siblings did you have? Where were you in the birth order?

11. What work/chores did you do as a child? As a teen?

12. When did you first come to see yourself as a leader? What were the circumstances?

13. Where did you learn basic social skills? How to relate to people? How to influence others?

14. What three important things did you learn from your father? From your mother?

15. Did your grandparents have a significant influence on your development? How?

16. Who were the primary influences on you as a child? As a teen? As a young adult?

17. What basic values were instilled in you as a child?

18. What leadership successes did you have in elementary school? Junior high? High school? College?

19. What mistakes did you make in your early leadership experiences? What did you learn from those?

20. To what/whom do you attribute your success as a leader?

21. What epitaph would you want on your tombstone? What legacy do you hope to leave?

22. What role has music had in your life?

23. What songs do you want sung at your funeral?

24. List five of the core values by which you live today.

25. What was your most painful experience as a child? As a teen? As a young adult? As an older adult?

26. Do you tend to avoid change or embrace it? Why?

27. Do you tend to avoid conflict or embrace it? Why?

28. What hobbies/leisure activities do you most enjoy?

29. What was the happiest time of your life? Most fulfilled? Most effective?

30. How do you manage money? Tend to spend or save? What are your giving patterns?

31. When and how did you come to faith in Christ?

32. When and how were you called to ministry?

33. What are the three primary principles by which you exercise your leadership?

34. Who else do you think I should interview for this book on the Ozarks and leadership?

Similarities of the Stories of Ozarkers

I found the similarities I shared with many of these remarkable. Most of the men, and some of the women, shared the common experience of putting up hay bales in the summer. Memories of the smell of fresh mown hay, the oppressive heat of barn lofts with tin roofs, and the relief of a dip in a stock tank or swimming hole after haying were shared by most.

Another favorite smell mentioned was the sweet smell of burlap sacks of dairy feed – a mixture of various grains and sorghum, designed to nurture cows and improve milk production. One mentioned waking up to the smell of bacon frying as his mother fixed breakfast before he went out to milk the cows. Another mentioned the smell of fresh-turned earth as he plowed behind a team of mules.

The importance of music was a recurring theme. Many came from families where strumming a guitar and singing hymns was a regular, if not a nightly, form of family entertainment. The influence of both Southern Gospel and Country music was a common bond for nearly all of us.

Every person I interviewed spoke of a deep faith that was nurtured by both church and home. Several became ministers; others became lay leaders in churches wherever they lived. Most gave credit to a very devout mother, dad or grandparent for that faith trajectory that guided their lives.

Leadership Development in the Ozarks

When I asked about the development of their leadership skills, Reverend Nolan Carrier shared his story as follows:

As a young boy growing up in a rural community, God used three venues to shape me and give me confidence to speak before a group of people. The first area where I gained experience and confidence as a "public speaker" took place every Sunday evening in an organization called Church Training. One hour before the Sunday evening worship at my home church, First Baptist in Lockwood, Missouri, I attended a class that taught church history, doctrine and polity. The adult leaders did not do the teaching, but each middle-elementary child would be given an assignment that was to be presented one week after it was made. The assignment was simply called "a part." We were to study our "part" and present it to the entire class of 10 to 15 other children. I took the assignment very seriously. I did not read it, as some children did, but I memorized it or made some short notes that I referred to during my five minute presentation. I got to where I looked forward to getting "a part" and presenting to the class.

I was also involved in our local 4-H club. (I still remember the 4-H's: Head, Heart, Hands and Health.) In each monthly meeting members would pledge the head to clearer thinking, hands to better service, heart to greater loyalty and health to better living. In 4-H, we signed up for projects that matched our passions and interests. There was an experienced adult leader who would guide the 4-Hers in their projects. That leader would teach on the subject, then members put into practice what they were taught. My passion was gardening. I loved to prepare a garden for planting. I enjoyed the planting and the care of a garden. It was a grand day when I was able to harvest vegetables from my garden and feed the family with these vegetables. I did very little to prepare the vegetables for consumption but I sure enjoyed the production part.

An important part of the project was to demonstrate to the entire club how to do a portion of the work. This presentation was simply called "A Demonstration." How I dreaded my first demonstration. I visited the "out-house" a couple of times before it was time for the presentation of my demonstration. You see, we met at a rural one-room school house and there was no inside restroom, so if you had to go, you had to go to the outhouse. And I did.

After just a couple of demonstrations before the entire Busy Bee 4-H Club, I gained confidence in speaking before a group and just like my church experience, looked forward to standing before my club to share how to do a particular part of my gardening project or beef project or cooking project.

The third venue God used to shape my life and prepare me for ministry was the Future Farmers of America organization in our local high school. In this organization I had many opportunities to develop leadership skills as well communication skills. I held an office in our FFA chapter. Because I was an officer I had the opportunity to work with the other officers of the chapter to plan and lead meetings. The chapter had many projects during the year. Officers were responsible to plan these projects and lead the entire chapter to carry out the responsibilities to complete the project. This was a skill that I would use weekly in ministry in the churches I pastored.

Whether it was the Church Council, Leadership Team, Deacon Committee or any number of other groups, there were projects and ministries to plan and supervise. The skills I learned in my high school FFA chapter came in handy in leading the church to accomplish its purposes.

I was also on the FFA livestock judging team. My father was a livestock judge and from the time I was 6 years old I would accompany my father to county fairs and watch him judge sheep, hogs and cattle. After every class that was shown, my father would go to a microphone and explain why he placed the class the way he did. I was impressed with his ability to think on his feet and speak boldly as he gave his reasons for judging the class the way he did.

In FFA I had the opportunity to do something similar. As a member of the livestock judging team we would judge a class of livestock. There would be four animals in the class. It was our responsibility to select the best animal in the group then the second best and third and fourth best. We then would stand before an adult judge and give our reasons for placing the class as we did. Those who were successful in giving "reasons" had to think on their feet, speaking logically, clearly and boldly.

Watching my father do this for ten or more years helped me to develop *this skill of judging livestock and giving "reasons." Later in ministry I would use these skills almost daily; the skills of "thinking on my feet", speaking with conviction, speaking clearly and boldly.*

God used church training in my local church, 4-H, and FFA to shape me for a teaching and preaching ministry that I have been involved in for close to fifty years.

Conclusion

Reverend Carrier, like everyone of my survey group, had some of his family heritage include the Scots-Irish blood spoken of earlier in this book. For most of them, it involved the immigration of ancestors from Ireland in the 18th century. Many of these ancestors had the experience of settling for a time in the Appalachian region, then later moving west and finding homes in the Ozarks.

My intention with the research was to identify common cultural influences that contributed to the leadership qualities of these Ozarkers. The rest of this book will examine those qualities and explore how they enabled effectiveness and significance in living and leading.

Chapter Three - Leadership Quality: Integrity

Clarity about Right and Wrong

"Integrity is doing the right thing even when no one is watching."
C. S. Lewis

One of the vivid memories of my pre-teen childhood is an occasion when I went with my Dad into Verona, the small town located about 5 miles from our farm, to purchase dairy feed at the general store in town. We called it the MFA Exchange. Towns all over Missouri had these franchises of the Missouri Farmers' Association that sold groceries, farm supplies, overalls, gloves, tractor parts, etc. We had canned vegetables from the garden and meat from the cow and hog we butchered and froze, and milk from the cows. But we bought sugar, flour, and other staples at the Exchange.

I remember a trip to town to buy three 100-pound bags of dairy feed. Dairy feed was an enriched mixture of grains designed to supplement the nourishment cows got from grazing and to improve their milk production. We made the routine trip, bought and loaded our gunny sacks of feed and started back home. About half-way there, Dad suddenly pulled the car over and stopped. He was obviously deep in thought, so I didn't say anything or ask why we were stopping. He reached into his pocket and pulled out several coins. He counted the coins and said, "Shorty gave me 50 cents too much in change."

He took off again, did a U-turn in the road, and headed back to town to return the extra change to the man at the Farmer's Exchange. I waited in the car while he took the 50 cents back and pondered what had just happened. I wondered, "Why go to that trouble to return 50 cents? Why not just wait till the next time you're in town to return it? Why not just consider it your good fortune and keep the 50 cents?"

What Dad taught me that day was that there is right and wrong. It is important to do right, and you don't want anyone to think, even for a moment, that you have taken advantage of them. Some would use the word "integrity." Dad (and Mom) taught me that integrity matters.

Most Ozarkers grew up hearing values taught through short, pithy sayings. Parents told their children, "Do what is right;" "Always keep your word;" "Don't lie, cheat or steal;" "Cheaters never win;" "You should only have what you work for." These teachings were usually backed up by a conscientious effort to set a good example by parents and grandparents.

In his book, *Ozark Country,* W. K. McNeil says that Ozarkers "invariably characterize their ancestors as honest, kind, and good people..." [18] All of those whom I interviewed spoke of a basic honesty – integrity - that characterized the lessons they learned from parents and grandparents.

Another way to describe this strong sense of right and wrong is as a passion for justice and a great hatred for injustice. That shows up nowhere more clearly in the history of the Ozarks than in the formation of the vigilante group called "the Bald Knobbers."

The Bald Knobbers and the Fight for Justice

The Bald Knobbers formed in the southern part of Missouri in 1885 and were active until 1889. They were given their name from the grassy bald summits of peaks in the Ozarks Mountains of Taney County where they had their meetings. In the post-Civil War period, the Bald Knobbers tended to be men who had sided with the North, and later they were opposed by the Anti-Bald Knobbers who were typically aligned with the South. But their existence was not primarily related to the Civil War.

The formation of the Bald Knobbers was originally about justice. Ozarks communities were largely lawless and wild societies. Being remote from cities with their law enforcement agencies, courts and judges, these communities tended to lack any dependable system of justice. There were numerous instances where local rowdies literally got away with murder. Where there was any semblance of law and order, it was very slow-moving and often corrupt.

In this vacuum of justice and fairness, a strong man arose as a leader. Nathaniel N. Kinney called a meeting of like-minded citizens. "The meeting grounds were on top of Snapp's Bald, a great treeless peak located about two miles northwest of Kirbyville, a village not far from the Kinney home... This particular peak commanded a view of the countryside that discouraged interlopers from drawing nearer than a half mile. Eavesdroppers could not hear what occurred atop the peak." [19]

The Bald Knobbers were a secretive group, often wearing hoods with horns, and they grew to include 100 to 200 men. The group was originally called a "law and order league, and enjoyed considerable support from the public." [20]

"One of the first significant actions taken by the Bald Knobbers was the lynching of two local rowdies that had terrorized local citizens and never been brought to justice. On April 15, 1885, the Bald Knobbers hanged Frank and Tubal Taylor in Taney County. News of the Taylor hangings flashed through Taney County like shock waves, vibrating across Southwest Missouri and into Arkansas. Citizens of nearby counties speculated about forming their own vigilante committees. At first the civic-minded folks of Taney County praised the Bald Knobbers' dramatic gesture as an act of good citizenship. Kinney and his vigilantes did society a favor, they said, ridding it of a couple of miscreants..." [21]

Over time the community changed its perception of the Bald Knobbers. An observer said, "What started out as an idealistic group of men dedicated to upholding the law, degenerated into a self-serving body of avengers, dedicated to settling personal feuds in the name of the clan." [22]

Eventually the Bald Knobbers were opposed both by local groups and by the state government. In response to alleged misdeeds of the Bald Knobbers, another group that came to be known as Anti-Bald Knobbers formed. By the Spring of 1986, the two groups were nearly at war in Taney County. Citizens of the area appealed to the Governor of Missouri to intervene and stop the shootings, beatings, and arson. On April 7,

1886, Governor Marmaduke demanded that Kinney disband the Taney County Bald Knobbers. [23]

On August 20, 1888, an Anti-Bald Knobber named Billy Miles assassinated Nathaniel Kinney. Billy and his brother Jim were tried for the murder, but acquitted on the grounds of self-defense. By 1890, the Bald Knobbers and the Anti-Bald Knobbers ceased to exist as organized vigilante groups in Southwest Missouri. But the controversy over who were the "good guys" and who were the "bad guys" of that era continued for generations. [24]

Regardless of how one views these citizen vigilante groups, they formed out of a desire to fight what people perceived as injustice. That desire for justice is nurtured by a deeply-imbedded sense of right and wrong that has been passed from one generation to another in the Ozarks.

Leadership and Trust

Those leaders whom I interviewed nearly unanimously affirmed that a part of their success as effective leaders was because people trusted them. The integrity with which they conducted their lives led people to believe that they were trustworthy.

Author and statesman Jim Webb has written extensively about the Scots-Irish heritage. In his book, *Born Fighting,* he says that this heritage, both by political and religious values, held that the individual had a "moral right to rebel against the unjust policies of any government. This concept...would form the basis for a more inclusive brand of populism first characterized by the presidency of Andrew Jackson." [25]

Populist presidents, who were not a part of the Eastern elite, have led the country from time-to-time, based largely on being perceived as persons who could be trusted. Often their flaws were obvious and beyond denial, but there was something about them that made them "likeable" or "trustworthy" in general perception. In most cases they came from rural settings and relative poverty. Other presidents who have shared Andrew Jackson's Scots-Irish heritage and populist appeal are: Jimmy Carter, Ronald Reagan and Bill Clinton. [26]

In closing his book, Jim Webb comments on the Scots-Irish willingness to fight for what is right. He says, "Who are we? We are the molten core at the very center of the unbridled, raw, rebellious spirit of America. We helped build this nation, from the bottom up. We face the world on our feet and not on our knees. We were born fighting. And if the cause is right, we will never retreat." [27]

Chapter Four

Leadership Quality: Family – Blood Ties and Clan

"Family is not an important thing, it is everything." Michael J. Fox

Family is important to Ozarkers. Family matriarchs and patriarchs are generally honored and respected. Both of my paternal grandparents were deceased by the time I was seven-years-old, so I have few memories of them. My Dad, the eldest of five brothers, "stood in" as the family patriarch, and my Mom as the designated hostess for family gatherings. Typically we had Thanksgiving and Christmas gatherings in the winter and wiener roasts over a bonfire in the summer, in addition to various birthdays, funerals, hog-butcherings, and other family events.

Grandpa Smith

On my mother's side, both grandparents lived well into my adulthood. Grandpa Sam Smith and his wife, Mary Foster Smith, hosted the annual family gathering at Christmas. My six sets of aunts and uncles on that side of the family usually gathered at mid-morning on Christmas in my grandparents' tiny house. Grandma prepared Christmas dinner on a wood stove, and we sat in the small kitchen and ate heartily. My cousins and I showed off what we got for Christmas and played with each others' new toys.

Grandpa Smith didn't have a car and lived modestly on his "Old Age Pension." When I was three or four living in Aurora, before the family moved to the farm, he often hitchhiked or walked the five miles from Marionville to Aurora to see me. He pulled me in my red wagon from our house on the north side to downtown to watch the amazing machinery at work through the big front window of the Coca-Cola bottling plant.

Grandpa Smith was thin and of average height, with a shock of white hair. Most of the time he wore a two or three day growth of beard. He loved his grandchildren and spent hours playing with them in his back yard where he fashioned toys out of tin cans and other discarded materials. He kept a large garden; grandma canned all kinds of produce. I don't recall many profound sayings from him, but I remember him as a gentle, loving man.

He had a particular word with which he began nearly every sentence. As a child, that word sounded to me like, "finymastakin." He said it as a single five-syllable word, and I heard it thousands of times. I was well into my teenage years before I finally figured out that he was saying, "if I ain't mistaken…" This humble man had developed the habit of making nearly every declarative statement with the admission that he could be wrong.

Grandpa was one of my best friends. Together we put out feed for the white squirrels that Marionville was known for. He took scrap tin and made airplanes with propellers that turned in the wind and cars with soda bottle caps for wheels. I was 20 when he died. Grandma Smith lived on for several years in the little house with the big garden out back, though the garden was never the same without grandpa's touch.

The Ozarkers whom I interviewed in researching this book shared similar stories of close family ties. Some had memories of families gathering around a piano or getting out guitars to sing hymns together in the evenings. Parents were generally given credit for providing discipline and teaching basic values in word and deed, but grandparents were often acknowledged as family leaders and respected sources of wisdom.

The Perry Boys in the Military

Grandpa Howard Perry died when my Dad was only 13-years-old. He had worked as a house painter and suffered through years of terrible headaches and what appeared to be "depression" before his early death. His family came to believe later that he died from lead poisoning due to his constant exposure to lead paint. At his death Dad became the man of the family; he missed one year of school working to help his mother make ends meet. He was disciplinarian for his mother with the four younger brothers. Oliver, being just a couple years younger than Dad and a strong and skilled fighter, became the one whom Dad could not whip with a peach tree switch after Oliver got to be a teenager.

When Dad and Oliver went into the army, Dad was glad for Oliver's fighting skills because it kept the two of them from being bullied by "street tough" guys who were drafted from big cities. Oliver, to this day at age 93, retains that toughness and willingness to stand up for what he thinks is right.

Their younger brother, Ray Perry, also joined the military and served during WW II. Brother Gene attempted to join the army but was found to have health issues that prevented his service. The youngest of the five Perry boys was Theodore, and he served in combat in the Korean Conflict and was awarded a Purple Heart.

Jim Webb traces this closeness of family ties back to the Scots-Irish traditions, as those immigrants came to the new world in 18th century. He says, "This 'Celtic tie of kinship' has survived in some form through the ages, even in America. An offshoot of this ancient concept defines the unusually strong feelings about military service held by so many Americans of Scottish and Irish descent, and helps explain why such a high percentage of American combat units in today's volunteer army are from Scots-Irish and Irish Catholic background." [28]

Brigadier General Waylen Jobe

Expressions of clan loyalty often take the form of fighting for the country and for one's brothers and sisters in arms. Several of the persons in my survey group were military veterans, but only one was a career soldier. Brigadier General Waylen Jobe of Willard, Missouri, served his country for over 32 years. Originally born and raised in Arkansas, he rose to the rank of General in 1984 by demonstrating extraordinary competence and unwavering loyalty to his country and to his troops.

During the Vietnam Conflict, General Jobe served at the National Guard Base in Springfield, Missouri, which specialized in helicopter repair. Once a month during those years, a cargo plane, such as a Lockheed C-130

Hercules, would fly in eight copters that had been shot up and damaged in Vietnam. The base had one month to get those eight serviced, repaired, and ready to go back into service. He made sure they were on their way back to Vietnam before the next group of eight arrived. General Jobe rose to be the commander of the base in Springfield, in addition to his having led engineer units in Korea and various bases in Europe. He is in the line of other outstanding soldiers from Missouri and Arkansas such as Generals John J. "Black Jack" Pershing, Omar Bradley, Douglas MacArthur, and Wesley Clark.

Family Feuds

The importance of family or clan in this culture was played out tragically in the infamous battles between the Hatfields and McCoys in the Appalachian Mountains. Family loyalty is a very strong value, and it means that family members fight for each other if necessary. The American military has been characterized by an emphasis on this "brother in arms" idea. Rather than depending on a blood tie, the clan becomes those with whom one shares a foxhole or a barracks.

In small towns and rural communities around the Ozarks, this history of fighting for the clan is well established. During the years I was in high school at Verona High, I travelled around southwest Missouri with our ball teams. We played sports in other small towns throughout the area, especially basketball and baseball. (Our school was too small and poor to field a football team.) Except Purdy, Missouri. Verona never played at Purdy and Purdy never played at Verona.

Why? I asked that question when I was a seventh-grader and noticed this incongruity. The answer I got from an upper-classman was that years before, at a basketball game with the Purdy team playing at the Verona gym, there was a brawl. A couple of the players got into a fist fight, and rather than fans or teammates rushing to the floor to break it up, they rushed to the floor to get in on the fight. A brawl ensued that would have been fit for a Wild West saloon. The upstanding citizens of Verona were going to fight for their boys. Grown men were held up as heroes, given credit for getting a blow in on one of those Purdy guys. So the athletic conference said, "No more games between Verona and Purdy."

Don't Sully the Family Name

When I was 15 I engaged in a teenage prank with a couple of my friends. Each year around the 4th of July the Lion's Club of Verona sponsored an annual picnic in the city park. There were carnival games, contests and entertainment of all kinds. The Lion's Club cooked hotdogs and hamburgers and sold soft drinks, as one of their annual fund raising events.

One of the games at the picnic was a dunking tank. This was a stock tank filled with water over which one of the Lion's Club members would sit on a hinged seat that was connected to a target. Contestants could buy 3 baseballs for a dollar to throw at the target, about a foot in diameter. When someone hit the target, it would trigger the hinged seat to collapse, and the person on the seat would get dunked in the tank. It was great fun, but we were looking for something more interesting that evening. Three of us went down to the general store and purchased a dozen eggs. We scattered ourselves through the crowd, and on a signal we each let fly with our four eggs at the Lion on the dunking seat.

There was a chain link barrier in front of the person over the tank so that he would not get hit accidentally by a baseball. When the eggs hit the chain link they splattered, and egg yolk flew all over the poor guy. Of course, all he had to do was jump in the tank to get cleaned off. After our little prank the three of us tried to keep a low profile and stay out of sight. Some of the Lion's Club members were searching for the ornery boys who did this.

While trying to stay out of sight, I overheard one of the searchers say, "I didn't see all of them, but one of them was that (expletive) kid of Bob Perry's." That statement struck me to the heart. My dad's legal name was Bob (not Robert), and I was known to everyone as Bobby. I realized that what I had done was not being blamed on me, it was being attributed to my dad. This man who spent his whole life trying to protect the family name and keep a good reputation was being held responsible in some minds for my stupidity. I had sullied the family name!

That incident did not keep me from ever committing another act of mischief, but it did cause me to think twice every time I was about to do something that might bring shame to the Perry name. A part of the Ozarks heritage is taking care of the family and protecting the community standing of the family name.

Nicknames

One of the ways in which community solidarity was indicated in many communities was that accepted and appreciated members of the community were given nicknames. In my little town those names were often related to either a particular preference or habit the person displayed or some aspect of their physical appearance. These nicknames were known by all and almost always used to refer to the person. Our town had wonderful characters nicknamed, "Spud," "Biscuit," "Jellybean," "Chief," "Banty," "Zippy," "Indian Joe," "Swede," "Boo," "Hog," "Moose," and "Bucky." The nickname was not always complimentary, but it was almost always a sign of acceptance in the community.

Loyalty is important. Loyalty to family. Loyalty to community. Loyalty to one's team. When Ozarkers come out of this culture to lead teams or organizations, they will be loyal to their team members and to the organization. They will defend those they perceive as friends or "family," and may sometimes be serious antagonists toward those they don't.

Chapter Five

Leadership Quality: Hard work - You Only Deserve What You Earn

"There is no substitute for hard work." Thomas Edison

Most Ozarkers who grew up before the latter third of the 20th century learned about hard work at an early age. It was a largely rural society, and even those who grew up in town rather than on a farm found themselves working on farms in the summer. Young people earned spending money by "bucking" hay bales (picking them up from the field and putting them on wagons), picking strawberries paid by the quart box, "detasseling" corn, or driving a tractor to plow, cultivate, mow or rake.

When teenage boys got old enough, some went to Kansas for the summer working in the wheat harvest. This involved long hours and hot, sweaty work. but a young man could make and save a fair amount of money if he didn't spend it on beer and partying on the weekends. Many a teenage boy came back from wheat harvest with enough money to buy his first used car. Some may have even saved some money for college later in their lives. Regardless of the goal, the work was hard and no one expected to receive anything he didn't earn by the sweat of his brow.

Working the Hay before Balers

Before the days when hay balers were commonly used, the job was even more work-intensive. One of my survey group, Patti Penny, tells about helping her grandfather on his farm near Seymour:

After we had raked the hay, my Grandfather would use a pitch fork and load the hay on a wagon. (In later years we got a hay loader which was a marvelous invention and reduced our work by half.) Once the hay was loaded, I would ride on top of the mound, and my Grandfather would drive the tractor to the barn. He had a hay fork that clamped down a load of hay to put in the barn loft. My job was to drive the tractor at the back of the barn to pull the hay up to the loft with a pulley system.

Well, on this occasion my little brother was visiting. He was about 3 years old, and he was standing at the back barn door watching me drive the tractor. He had his hand on the pulley rope and was "helping" me pull the hay in the loft. All of a sudden the hay hit the track in the loft and the rope pulled his hand into the pulley. Complete chaos erupted. He was screaming and crying. I finally got his hand out of the pulley and he took off running to the house. We finally got him in the pickup and drove him to the Mansfield Hospital where they stitched up his hand. He is 66 years old, and you can still see the scar. Of course we have told the story a million times. It was certainly one of the more traumatic moments in my life.

In those years everything took more time and harder work than we expect today. Felling and cutting up trees with a crosscut saw was much more time consuming and labor intensive than doing it with a chainsaw. Butter didn't come from the dairy case in the supermarket; it was churned from the rich milk of a Jersey cow, and that took time. The house wasn't warmed because of a thermostat on the wall; it came from hours of cutting and stacking wood, bringing it in to the potbelly stove in the living room and lighting a fire before daylight.

Chores to Dislike Intensely

There were two particular jobs on our 80-acre farm that I hated. One was picking up rocks. Dad would have me spend hours in the summers picking up rocks and tossing them in a tractor-drawn wagon to be put in a large pile at one corner of the field or in a nearby "draw" or valley. There were two kinds of farmers around us. Some had bottom land near a river or creek with rich, fertile topsoil; some had hilltop or hilly land with rocks held together by dry, dusty soil that mostly wanted to grow brush and weeds. We had the hilly land.

No matter how clear of rocks I managed to get a particular plot of land, after the field was plowed or went through a strong rain, a new "crop" of rocks appeared. The rocks varied from the size of a golf ball to the size of a volleyball, and trying to eliminate rocks from an Ozarks field came to epitomize the ultimate waste of time and energy.

The other job I disliked was cleaning the barn. Cleaning the barn was our euphemism for shoveling cow manure. A gutter ran through the barn. As the cows were put in stanchions for milking, they could be fed at one end and do their business into the gutter at the other end. Our cows seemed better at producing feces than milk. Those gutters had to be shoveled to the outside of the barn into a giant pile. After the manure pile weathered and dried a few weeks, the manure was pitched-forked into a wagon to be spread on the land as fertilizer. By that time it was less stinky, so the task was less unpleasant. These jobs taught me the necessity of hard work and pointed me toward getting enough education so that I would not be shoveling s*** the rest of my life.

Hard work was not a new concept for Ozarkers. Early European-origin settlers came to these hills to work hard, tilling rocky soil, surviving hot, dry summers and scraping a poverty-level subsistence from small farms. Most of the "common-folk" farmers had 80 to 120 acres of land – barely enough to raise cattle and crops sufficient to survive. My Dad, and most of the small farmers had to have jobs "in town" to supplement their farming income. In some cases their wives also worked at salaried jobs to keep the family going.

In his book, *An Hour Before Daylight: Memories of a Rural Boyhood*, former President Jimmy Carter writes about the hard work that was part of his experience on a Georgia farm. He says, "It seemed natural for white folks to cherish our Southern heritage and cling to our way of life, partially because the close ties among many of our local families went back another hundred years before the war, when our Scotch-Irish ancestors had come to Georgia from the British Isles or moved south and west, mostly from Virginia and the Carolinas." [29] The title of his book highlights the strong work ethic that involved getting up early in the morning to start the work day. Carter's ancestors settled in Georgia rather than winding up in Arkansas or Missouri, but he traces them to the same Scots-Irish stock that migrated from Virginia and the Carolinas. Their strong work ethic went back to hard-scrabble farming and sweat-of-the-brow lifestyles in Scotland and Ireland.

No Shortcuts to Prosperity

In recent decades many in the Ozarks have become distressed with the coming of lotteries and casinos. Their objection is not just a moral one based on opposition to gambling. It also violates the ethos that says that you should acquire only that which you earn. Money secured by winning a lottery or a game of blackjack violates this direct relationship between work and gain. Likewise, Ozarkers are loathe to accept a handout from others, whether charity or government, if they are able to work and support themselves.

The men and women who grew up in this culture learned to "do their chores." Doing chores implies that the task at hand may not be something one **wants** to do, but it is something that **has to be done.** For a leader, this teaches the internal discipline that causes him or her to be consistent in doing the work: the leader shows up for work. The leader thus is more likely to not ask others to do jobs he or she is not willing to do him or herself.

Hard work was a common thread among all of those Ozarkers whom I interviewed. Most of them did farm work that included milking cows and working the land. They learned a way of life that depended on their own hard work and the providence of God in sending the rain and sunshine to make things grow. Those two principles became the essence of life: you work hard; you trust the Lord.

Chapter Six – Leadership Quality: Creativity

Fix It with Baling Wire and Binder Twine

"Creativity is intelligence having fun." Albert Einstein

Ozarkers have a cultural propensity for fixing things. They are not afraid to tinker with something, take it apart, put it back together and hope it works. One of the things I discovered among the people I interviewed was a large number for whom math was a favorite subject in high school. Many of them majored in math in college and several became math teachers. A strong part of the Ozarks heritage is figuring things out, solving problems, and making do with what is available.

Creating Out of Nothing

During my growing up years in the 1950s and 1960s, hay balers bound the compacted hay with rough hemp or sisal cords usually called "binder twine" or "baler twine." All farms where hay was fed to cattle had an abundance of used binder twine. Every time a hay bale was opened to be fed to cattle, the two pieces of twine that wrapped the long dimension of the rectangular bale were saved. On the farm, that twine was saved in large balls that accumulated in the barn to be used for all kinds of projects where some kind of rope or string was needed.

In earlier years, those bales had been held together with wire. Baling wire likewise was kept and stored as bales were opened, and every self-respecting farmer had stores of wire lying around, even years after wire bales were discontinued. Many things that needed to be fixed, tied up or held together were given the creative application of binder twine or baling wire. (These were the days before duct tape was commonplace and became the new binder twine.)

My dad carried a good supply of baling wire in the tool box on the side of the tractor. When something broke on the tractor or on an implement out in the field, the fix very often was the innovative use of a pair of pliers and a length of baling wire. I have several antique mantle clocks in my house that my dad reclaimed from ruin. He beautifully refinished the wooden boxes, usually oak, and he tinkered with and repaired the works. I can show you several places in a couple of those clocks where dad used a piece of baling wire to replace a missing part. That takes some creativity.

Chuck Williams

Dr. Chuck Williams was a high school and college basketball star from Buffalo, Missouri. He carried the nickname "the Springfield Rifle" when he played for Missouri State University because of his phenomenal long-distance jump shot. His college roommate in the athletic dorm was Curtis Perry, who went on to a distinguished NBA career with the Milwaukee Bucks and the Phoenix Suns.

Chuck had a successful career as a college basketball coach and educator. He was one of those who studied math and learned from that discipline that "problems can be solved." He described his father as a life-long learner who, when presented with a challenge said, "We can fix this!" Chuck credits this problem solving approach to his ability to build successful teams and develop winning strategies.

Hosea Bilyeu

Another math learner who became a high school math teacher before being called to Christian ministry is Hosea Bilyeu. The name Hosea (pronounced "Ho-zee") has been in the family for 170 years, always with that spelling and pronunciation. Hosea became a pastor and built a large church in Springfield, Missouri. He believes that one of his early lessons from his parents was that "it was all right to try something and fail." His parents gave him permission to risk, with the understanding that if he failed with one effort, he could learn from that and try something else. That willingness to risk allowed Hosea to attempt many creative ventures for the benefit of his church and community.

Some years ago, when many in the Springfield area were bemoaning the existence of a large western-theme bar and entertainment venue called "Remington's," Hosea led his church to approach the owners of the facility with an offer to purchase. The place formerly known for drunkenness, drug use and parking lot brawls, was bought and became a wholesome place available for family events. Remington's today is a venue for community blood drives, charitable events, benefit concerts, and all kinds of activities that make the community a better place to live. Problem solved.

Vernon Armitage

A part of creativity is also found in curiosity. Ozarkers often look at something complex and wonder how it works. They consider the future and are curious about how it might be impacted by various scenarios. Vernon Armitage grew up at Chestnut Ridge, Missouri, a small community in the Ozarks Mountains not far from Branson. His father owned and operated a general store.

Vernon watched his dad and worked alongside him as the entrepreneur expressed curiosity about whether he should add tire sales to his line of groceries, feed and farm supplies. Later he added furniture and electrical supplies. The store became a center of the community because it carried so many items that people previously had to drive the 40-or-so miles to Springfield to buy. Vernon took that entrepreneurial spirit to his work as a pastor and built Pleasant Valley Baptist Church in the Kansas City area from a church of 100 attendees to over 4,000 in the 40 years he led that congregation.

Patti Penny

One of the outstanding entrepreneurs in the Ozarks is Mrs. Patti Penny. Patti grew up on a farm near Seymour, Missouri. She was the product of a broken home and was largely raised by her grandparents on their dairy farm. Her family knew poverty and challenges of all kinds.

Her grandmother taught her, "Patti, you can do anything." She took that confidence to school and became a leader in elementary school and on into high school. She had a great love for organizing things and making things happen. After working for several business enterprises in Springfield, in 1988 she started Penmac Staffing Services, Inc. It soon became a large, multi-state personnel placement service. Patty created a corporate giant that provides added value for hundreds of persons and companies around the country.

Bob Dale

Dr. Robert Dale is a professor, author and consultant who grew up at Neosho, Missouri. He started as a farm boy who became an engineering major and went on to study theology, psychology and organizational behavior. His books on leadership have been widely read and helped an entire generation of non-profit leaders. He is a visionary who helps organizations anticipate the kind of world that is coming, and he values his Ozarks upbringing. Bob's son Cass Dale followed in his dad's footsteps and is an accomplished futurist who specializes in studying religious terrorism.

Crafting Products and People

Curiosity, problem-solving, fixing it with what is available – all of those involve creativity, and creativity is a part of the culture of the Ozarks. The craftsmanship of the Ozarks is celebrated at Silver Dollar City, near Branson, and at scores of craft stores and museums throughout the Ozarks. W. K. McNeil, in *Ozark Country,* says, "For at least a century and half many kinds of musical instruments have been produced by Ozark craftsmen. These include fiddles, banjos, guitars, hammered dulcimers, mountain dulcimers, and others... Probably the most famous craft product created in the Ozarks is the wooden johnboat...The johnboat is a long, narrow, flat-bottomed boat designed for fishing the pools of Ozark rivers and for floating over the swift, shallow streams." [30]

Ozarks creativity shows in the accomplishments of local writers, musicians, entrepreneurs and inventors through the years. Among these are Rose O'Neill who created the Kewpie doll and lived at her home called Bonniebrook, in Taney County, Missouri. The famous artist, Thomas Hart Benton was a native of Neosho, Missouri. Jimmie Driftwood, who wrote the song, "The Battle of New Orleans" lived on a farm near Timbo, Arkansas.

Country music singer Porter Wagoner began his career at West Plains, Missouri. Laura Ingalls Wilder lived in Mansfield, Missouri, and wrote her *Little House on the Prairie* and other bestsellers there. Sam Walton, founder of Wal-Mart Stores, was born in Oklahoma but lived in Missouri and Arkansas towns. His ancestors can be traced back to Webster County, MO.

Today's child of the Ozarks has this impressive heritage of ancestors who applied their baling wire and binder twine problem-solving skills to accomplish great things. Present and coming generations are destined to produce scientists, researchers, inventors, authors and entrepreneurs who will have a positive impact on our world.

Chapter Seven – Leadership Quality: Storytelling

Embellishing Isn't Lying

"People are hungry for stories. It's part of our very being. Storytelling is a form of history, of immortality too. It goes from one generation to another." Studs Terkel

Effective leaders communicate effectively with their constituencies, with their staff members, and with the general public. For Ozarkers an important element of that communication is in the telling of stories. Like our ancestors sitting around a campfire in Scotland or Ireland, storytelling serves as an effective way for us to teach, inspire and share a culture.

Storytelling is an important part of Ozarks lore and culture. These are often stories of "weather, deception, crime, sacrifice, love, hate, historic adventures, and so on. And stories of poverty, which the Ozarks cannot avoid and do not try to avoid..." Weather stories tend to be related to drought, tornados and flooding. [31] People tell stories about the things that impact their lives and the people who inhabit their world.

Grandpa's Poke

Sometimes the stories are told with the particular vocabulary and grammar of the Ozarks. The dialects of the Ozarks reflect unique usage of language. Many old-timers referred to a paper bag as a "poke." My own grandpa Sam Smith gave each of us grandkids a "poke" (small brown bag) with candy and chips when we visited his house in Marionville.

He kept a wooden box under his bed, which I later learned was an ammunition box from World War I. He stocked his box with wrapped candy, potato chips, and other goodies. When the family was about to leave from a visit, grandpa would say, "Wait till I get your poke," then would go into the bedroom, close the door, and put together the poke for each kid. He did that with every grandchild at every visit. I have that box in my living room now, and it's filled with toys for the children who visit us.

People in the Ozarks often applied an "est" to words to turn a verb into an adjective, i.e. he was the "preachin'est preacher" or the "travellin'est traveler." Ozarkers often called a woodpecker a "peckerwood." The woodpecker is considered to be a pest and or nuisance, so like other words sharing a similar context (a nuisance, bother, pest, etc.), it quickly became a common retort in social circles and groups of friends. To be called a "peckerwood" was not a compliment. If something was not quite straight or level, it might be called "wauperjawed" or "catawampus." Everyone who grew up in the Ozarks understood those words, and there was no need for translation.

Tall Tales

Many tall tales in the Ozarks involved hunting and fishing. Here is example from W. K. McNeil: "One day an old hillbilly went fishing. He really had hung one and was having a big battle getting it to the top. Just as he was about to get it in the boat, the old catfish gave a heave and knocked the hillbilly's glasses off as it escaped. About a year later the old fellow was fishing in about the same place as before when he hooked a big one. When he landed the fish, it turned out to be the same one he had hooked last year. He knew because the fish was wearing his glasses." [32]

Another example of a tall tale, also recorded by W. K. McNeil in his book, *Ozarks Mountain Humor*, goes: "I heard of a dog in southern Arkansas that was so smart that any time his master got out his shotgun he started sniffing the ground in search of quail. But if his master grabbed a rifle he started searching the trees for squirrels. Once his master started fishing. The dog took a look at the rod and reel and tore out. Sure enough they found him digging worms. [33]

Embellishing Isn't Lying

In the Ozarks, lying was considered a serious moral violation. People depended on the good word of those with whom they made agreements. But "the tall tale" was a different matter. Tall tales have been acceptable and popular in the Ozarks throughout its history. A tall tale is a story so ridiculous or incredible that the reasonable listener should know that it is not intended to be taken literally. [34]

The kind of exaggeration or embellishment that made a tall tale was part of the charm and entertainment quality of the story. Sometimes the embellishment was obvious; sometimes it was more subtle. The good storytellers could shift imperceptibly from the ridiculous tall story to the embellished true story to the factually accurate story, and listeners were left to their own wits to distinguish among them.

Mike Haynes Family Story

Dr. Mike Haynes, a longtime pastor and church association director in the Ozarks, grew up in northeast Oklahoma. He shares a family story about how his grandfather stood up for what he believed to be right and just.

My Granddad worked for an oil company in the 1930s and 40s taking care of a pipeline that ran from Oklahoma City to St. Louis along a route parallel to old US Highway 66. His family moved up and down that pipeline living much of the time in southwest Missouri. After many years of doing this, he decided to settle more permanently in Chelsea, Oklahoma, where he opened a gas station and convenience store. His business in Chelsea was doing great until there developed talk in the 1960s of building what would become the Will Rogers Turnpike. It would be a very limited access toll road, and it would bypass most of the smaller towns along its route. The plans called for the town of Chelsea to be bypassed by several miles. This meant that Granddad's gas station, as well as most of the other small businesses in town, would be severely damaged.

The local merchants had a series of meetings to talk about how to keep Chelsea alive by making sure the turnpike ran near the town and had an access and exit nearby. At one of those meetings a leading town father said, "We can keep this disaster from happening to our town. We just need to go to Oklahoma City with some money and ply our state representatives with 'wine, women and song' to get them to see things our way."

When the town leader talked about "bribing" politicians with "wine, women and song" granddad took the floor and said, "You, sir, have crossed a line with me. I will have no part of supporting anything that is immoral. As much as I love our town and my business, I won't have my name associated with what you are talking about."

As it turned out, the town was bypassed and granddad had to close his business. However, his entrepreneurial spirit came through, and he started other successful enterprises. This story has passed down through our family as a lesson to challenge all of us to stand up for what is right. Granddad took on a town patriarch and paid a price to stand for his principles. Those of us who came after have tried to follow his example.

My Dad's Teenage Adventure

Most Ozarks families had stories and storytellers who would repeat the stories over and over to family members and friends in different settings. One of my Dad's stories was about his great adventure traveling to the west coast and back. When he finished high school, and before he went into the army during World War II, he had a great adventure. Missouri was still feeling the effects of the Depression, and jobs were hard to find. He had an uncle in Oregon who offered him a job in construction if he could get out there. His mother, a single mom with four boys younger than Dad, helped him come up with enough train fare to get to Oregon. He was to work for the uncle, keep enough of his pay to get by, and send the rest home to his mother to help support the family.

When he arrived in Oregon, the uncle said, "Sorry, but the construction business has really slowed down, and I don't have a job for you." At that point Dad had no choice but to go back home to south Missouri, but he didn't have bus or train fare. He started out with a small amount of money for food and began hitchhiking across Oregon. It was slow going, but he came into contact with a friendly "hobo" who offered to help him get back to the Midwest.

The hobo showed Dad how to hop eastbound freight cars and gave him an education on survival in that world. He first advised Dad to hide what little money he had in his shoe so that anyone on a boxcar who tried to rob him in his sleep would be less likely to find and take it. Then as they rode toward Billings, Montana, the hobo had them get off the train and walk around town to catch another eastbound train. The hobo said that there was a training center for the Railroad Police in Billings, and they always inspected boxcars that rolled into the Billings rail yard. They would arrest vagrants, sentence them to 30 days, and put them on a work detail for the County. When the sentence was served, before the person could get out of town, they would likely be rearrested and sentenced to another 30 days of hard labor. That could go on for a long time.

None of us ever knew how true the hobo's stories were, but we believed every detail Dad told us. He said that he finally reached somewhere in Kansas and found he had enough money left in his shoe to actually buy a train ticket to get the rest of the way home. After he got home he joined the CCC (Civilian Conservation Corps), one of the programs President Frankin Roosevelt initiated in order to put unemployed young men to work doing community improvement projects. Dad had more adventures in the CCC as he met and interacted with young men from other cultures. Then came the army and his service in Europe during the war. Like many veterans, he almost never talked about combat experiences, but he did tell stories about the sights he saw and the people he met.

These stories are a part of our family culture, and the idea of seeing new places and experiencing new adventures became an inspiration for me as a boy to want to see the world beyond the Ozarks. I lived and worked in Mexico City, Guadalajara and Oaxaca, Mexico. I lived in Washington, D. C. and Richmond, Virginia. I have been privileged to travel extensively to places all over the world. I owe my dad and some of his brothers for the yen for adventure and travel that was a part of my family system.

I enjoyed all of the far-flung places I lived and traveled, but there was also another impulse implanted from my family system. When it came time to retire, I was drawn back to the beautiful hills and clear springs of the Ozarks. I live on eight acres where my office window looks out on the woods behind the house and the occasional deer, turkeys, squirrels or rabbits that run through the clearing. I love this quiet life in the Ozarks, but I have adventure stories to tell my grandchildren.

Chapter Eight – Leadership Quality: Storytelling in Music

We Sing our Stories

"Music is a world within itself, with a language we all understand."
Stevie Wonder

The storytelling heritage that made its way to the Ozarks in the 19th century took musical form. When the telling of the story was put to music, it resulted in what is broadly called "the ballad." Scotland and Ireland, and later the Appalachians, produced songs that told stories. This style of singing contributed heavily to the development of country music and southern gospel music in the United States.

According to Wikipedia, "a ballad is a form of verse, often a narrative set to music… Ballads were particularly characteristic of the popular poetry and song of the British Isles from the later medieval period until the 19th century and used extensively across Europe and later the Americas."

The songs tell the stories of failed love affairs, broken hearts, tractors, pickup trucks, hangovers and honkie tonks. At church and in revival meetings the songs are testimonials about sin and redemption, obedience and rebellion, and heaven and hell. The songs tell the "old, old, story," and they tell the first-person contemporary story of one's experience of God.

Singing Ozarkers

Music played an important part in the lives of most of the persons I interviewed for this book. Hosea Bilyeu plays the guitar and sings, and his family does concerts of gospel music throughout the year in a variety of venues. Members of the Bilyeu family and various "in-laws" have long been a part of the country music scene in Branson, Missouri. Vernon Armitage plays the guitar and sings and was a part of a widely known gospel group called "The Waymakers" during his high school and college years (which group also included some of the Bilyeu family).

Bill Rowe, the retired baseball coach and Athletic Director of Missouri State University, grew up with music filling the atmosphere of Buck Prairie Baptist Church during his childhood and youth. His love of gospel music has continued through the years.

Ann Ashcraft, a minister's spouse who grew up at Neosho, Missouri, has served as an educator in both religious and secular settings. A significant influence in her life was hearing her father sing with a gospel quartet that toured throughout Missouri and Arkansas as she was growing up. Bob Dale, also from Neosho, recalls his father organizing and promoting gospel music concerts featuring nationally known quartets such as the Blackwood Brothers and the Statesmen.

Russell Newport

One of the most notable musicians from the Ozarks is Russell Newport. He grew up at Buffalo, Missouri, where his father owned a grocery store and a hardware store. Russell went on to own and operate a string of variety stores in various towns in the Ozarks. During World War II, Russell served as an officer aboard a Destroyer in the U. S. Navy.

Russell's mother was a pianist and vocalist, and she began teaching him both of those very early. In high school, he was given voice lessons by Chester Moffat for 3 years. Later he was taken to Southwest Baptist College in Bolivar and Drury College in Springfield for advanced voice training. He went on to study voice at William Jewell College in Liberty, Missouri. While in the Navy he sang with a large church choir in San Francisco, and he organized a band of his fellow sailors aboard the ship.

After the war, Russell used his G. I. Bill benefit to pursue a Master's degree in Business Administration at Harvard University. While studying business at Harvard, he also studied voice for two and one half years at the New England Conservatory of Music. Russell became a world-renowned tenor.

At the same time he was running his businesses and leading the music at First Baptist Church in Springfield, he spent 20 years touring the world doing concerts. He sang in Europe, Japan, Korea and throughout the

United States, including an appearance on the Ed Sullivan Show. His records and CDs have blessed people throughout the world.

I had the privilege of singing in Russell's choir at First Baptist Church in Springfield as a college student in 1962 and 1963, and I watched his appearance on the Ed Sullivan show with great excitement. He served as the "temporary" minister of music at the church for 15 years. Today Russell is 93-years-of-age, and he is still singing. His music tells the stories that are meaningful to him, and his singing allows those stories to touch the hearts of thousands.

Russell is a classically trained musician; his music is not the kind of music played on most radio stations in the area. He is a critically-acclaimed and widely respected tenor. But his love of music and his ability to phrase and express music that touches the heart were developed in the Ozarks.

Country and Southern Gospel Music

Author and Statesman Jim Webb notes that country and gospel music have been developed by musicians who share a common cultural heritage. Scots-Irish musicians include Elvis Presley, Johnny and June Carter Cash, the Carter family, Hank Williams, and many others. The heart of country music found its way from Ireland, and it often includes patriotic as well as religious themes. [35] As a matter of fact, you could name many well-known country artists before you would name one who did not have some of the Scots-Irish heritage.

That historic strand is beautifully documented in the novel, *The Songcatcher,* by Sharyn McCrumb. This novel traces the movement of folk music from a Scottish Island to the Appalachian Mountains of western North Carolina. It shows how Irish and Scottish immigrants to America brought the songs that became the heart of Country music. A film by the same name dramatizes that history and features many of those early mountain folk tunes. [36]

The Ozarks involvement in telling our stories in music has not been limited to just "picking and singing," however. "For at least a century and half, many kinds of musical instruments have been produced by Ozarks craftsmen. These include fiddles, banjos, guitars, hammered dulcimers, mountain dulcimers, and others." [37] Those hand-crafted instruments are featured and sold at stores thought the Ozarks, especially at Silver Dollar City, near Branson, Missouri. The guitar has long been a favorite and most common instrument, and many Ozarkers learn to play at least a few chords as a part of their growing up in the area.

Blue Grass Music and Nolan Carrier's Story

Nolan Carrier is a long-time pastor of churches in the Ozarks, having served churches in Windsor, Ava and Springfield, Missouri. Here is a story of how music has had a deep influence on his life:

I grew up on a farm outside Lockwood, Missouri. I spent many hours throughout my growing up working with my dad on our farm. I was very involved in both 4-H and FFA during those years, and those involvements taught me a great deal about hard work, discipline and leadership.

When my mother passed away on December 3, 2005, and my dad passed away on March 29, 2006, I led both of their funerals. Having been a pastor for many years, and having done hundreds of funerals in that capacity, it did not seem difficult at the time for me to do this. We celebrated their lives and the fact that they had gone home to be with the Lord.

I think preachers often suppress their emotions so that they can lead funerals and minister to families without breaking down. In this case I did not allow myself to weep or feel deep emotion about losing my parents. Years later someone recommended to me the excellent Blue Grass music written and performed by the Gibson Brothers.

As I listened to their song, "The Farm of Yesterday," I found myself feeling the depth of my loss as I remembered my times of being with parents on our farm. The words of the song washed over me, and I relived some of those times riding in the pickup with my dad. I recalled the times we baled hay and put it up in the barn. The song touched me more deeply than anything I had felt since the death of my parents. It allowed me to more fully remember and grieve my experiences on that "farm of yesterday."

Here are the lyrics of "The Farm of Yesterday" by the Gibson Brothers:

Sideburns a little long,
Red Man hat and country songs
On a.m. radio
In a pickup truck behind the cows
driving them to pasture

How I miss those mornings so
Seated to the right hand of a hard-working man
Our backs against the border every day
Staring at the prairie to the south
I'd fill my mouth
With breakfast on that farm of yesterday

We'd see our mother's smile
light the home place all the while
Through good times and bad
Happy with her lot in life proud
to be farmer's wife

It makes me kind of sad
To think our father always felt
that he had let us down
When times were tough and farming didn't pay
He should known we saw him
as a king and we still do
In memories of that farm of yesterday

They build 'em bigger now
They got more land, they got more cows
Maybe they have found a better way
It's hard to say
But I miss that old farm of yesterday

61

I woke the other day
Tired from dreams of stacking hay
And picking stubborn stones
Fifty years and miles away
That farm of yesterday has not left me alone

I think memories make a man
What he will always be
And I'm not sure what I am trying to say
But if there's anything I can add
To this old world
It's thanks to that old farm of yesterday

They build 'em bigger now
They got more land, they got more cows
Maybe they have found a better way
It's hard to say
But I miss that old farm of yesterday

Favorite Hymns in the Ozarks

The songs people choose as "favorites," and the songs that endure through the decades indicate the heart-felt values of a group of people. Themes and central messages of these hymns reveal core values of the culture. Some churches have had a tradition of informal periods of singing, perhaps on a Sunday night, when people request their favorites. Here are two of those that are most requested:

"Amazing Grace" is known by almost everyone. Even persons who have long-since stopped going to church still seem to know and love the hymn. The words say:

Amazing grace! How sweet the sound,
that saved a wretch like me!
I once was lost, but now am found,
was blind, but now I see.

'Twas grace that taught my heart to fear,
and grace my fears relieved;
how precious did that grace appear
the hour I first believed.

Through many dangers, toils, and snares,
I have already come;
'tis grace hath brought me safe thus far,
and grace will lead me home.

When we've been there ten thousand years,
bright shining as the sun,
we've no less days to sing God's praise
than when we first begun.

The first two stanzas express the composer's (John Newton), and the singer's testimony of coming to salvation through the experience of God's grace. The story then shifts in the third stanza to how God has shown his grace by keeping us safe in spite of the difficulties of life. Finally, the song celebrates the belief in an eternity in heaven that awaits those who love God. Those themes of salvation, abundant life and heaven are oft-repeated in favorite hymns in the Ozarks.

Another widely-popular gospel song is "How Great Thou Art." This song was made prominent as George Beverly Shea sang it in Billy Graham Crusades throughout several decades, and it continues to be enjoyed in recordings by dozens of artists. The song's lyrics are:

O Lord my God! When I in awesome wonder
consider all the worlds Thy hands have made,
I see the stars, I hear the rolling thunder,
Thy power throughout the universe displayed.

(Chorus) - Then sings my soul, my Savior God, to Thee;
How great Thou art, how great Thou art!
Then sings my soul, my Savior God, to Thee;
How great Thou art, how great Thou art!

When through the woods and forest glades I wander,
and hear the birds sing gently in the trees;
When I look down from lofty mountain grandeur,
and hear the brook and feel the gentle breeze;

(Chorus)

And when I think that God, His Son not sparing,
sent him to die, I scarce can take it in;
That on the cross, my burdens gladly bearing,
He bled and died to take away my sin.

(Chorus)

When Christ shall come with shout of acclamation,
and take me home, what joy shall fill my heart!
Then I shall bow in humble adoration,
and there proclaim, "My God, how great thou art!"

(Chorus)

This hymn begins with an acknowledgement of God's work in creating a beautiful world. It celebrates the stars, thunder, woods, glades, birds, mountains, brooks and the breeze. For Ozarkers singing about the wonders of nature resonates with their appreciation of the natural beauty they see in their environment. The third stanza shifts to a testimony about God's provision of salvation through the death of Christ. Finally, the hymn shifts to the theme of heaven and the joy of eternity. It tells a complete story of the earthly experience and the heavenly home.

You Are Singing My Story – the Authors' Experience

There have been times when a song spoke to me in ways that mere words could not. I hear country songs that seem to describe experiences I have been through, and I identify with the emotions expressed. Gospel music provides me with ways to express my own faith journey and celebrate my own relationship with God. As powerful as storytelling is as a method of communication, it becomes even more powerful when set to music.

Chapter Nine – Leadership Quality: Humor

Laughter is More than Good Medicine

"Through humor you can soften some of the worst blows that life delivers. And once you find laughter, no matter how painful your situation may be, you can survive." Bill Cosby

Great leaders are able to utilize humor to motivate, persuade, and encourage those they work with. Humor can calm a situation of conflict, disarm a critic, and drive home a point in a debate. Ozarkers are blessed with a culture that is rich in humor. Among the persons I interviewed, are educators, military leaders, preachers, coaches and entrepreneurs. All of them possess keen senses of humor.

Paul Swadley

One in my survey group was Reverend Paul Swadley. This longtime Ozarks pastor made use of humor as well as anyone I have been able to discover. Rev. Swadley spent 25 years as pastor of South Haven Baptist Church in Springfield, Missouri, and after his retirement he served 10 churches as an interim pastor. "Swad," as friends call him, says that he got his sense of humor from his father, who was also an Ozarks preacher. He says, "If you can get people to laugh, they will hear you."

I co-officiated a wedding with Swad several years ago, and as the groom and his attendants gathered with the ministers in a side room before going out for the ceremony, there was clearly a great deal of nervousness in the room. Swad looked at the groom and said, "Well, Mike, you are getting a fine girl as a wife today." Mike replied, "Yes, I know that." Swad said, "Frankly, a lot of us thought she could have done a lot better." Everyone laughed, the tension eased, and the groom and his men filed out of the room with smiles on their faces.

In his years of ministry, Swad's records indicate that he performed 1,039 weddings. I learned later that he used the same or a similar line about "she could have done better" with nearly every one of those grooms. His sermons were sprinkled with down-home Ozarks humor and vernacular.

The Greene County Sheriff visited South Haven and was seated way in the back in an overflow room. Swad was reading visitor's cards at the end of the service, as the visitors each stood. He stumbled over the card, "Michell ?, Mitchell? Mi . . ." The people in the choir were saying, "It's Mickey Owen, the sheriff." Swad said, "Oh, it's Mickey Owen, our sheriff. Well, Mr. Owen, I sure hope you can shoot straighter than you can write."

Here is one of Swad's oft-told stories in his own words:

When I was a boy we moved from the Shelton place over to the Oren Bloomer place, and I attended the Elm Grove School. Our teacher's name was Leo Pigg. I am not making this up. We did live on the Bloomer place. I did go to Elm Grove School, and our teacher WAS Mr. Leo Pigg. In this school, in fact in almost every grade school, there was one person who was a tattle tale. They would just run and tell the teacher everything. And usually in those one room schools, there was a cry baby. You could just point a finger at them and they would start crying. Well, at Elm Grove School, there was a girl by the name of Wilda Mae Wolf, and she was both. The rest of us just couldn't stand her.

Now when I was in eighth grade, the thing I wanted most was a bicycle. Every night I would pray for a new bicycle. I told God if he would just get me a new bicycle, I'd never ask for anything else as long as I lived. I was lying, but I didn't know I was lying, because I wanted it so bad. On December 6, 1941, my Dad went to Springfield to Montgomery Ward and bought me a new Hawthorne Bicycle - red with white stripes. Prettiest thing I ever saw in my life. Now almost everybody knows what happened on December 7, 1941, but on Monday, December 8th I wasn't interested in Pearl Harbor. I got up before anybody, went to the barn and got my chores done way early, because I was determined to be the first person on the school grounds at Elm Grove. I wanted every body to see my new bicycle.

My best friend was Clarence Stark, and I didn't think he was ever going to get there that day, but finally he came. He said, 'Swad, can I ride it?' I said, 'Sure.' We pushed the bike up to the top of the hill and he got on it. Now he'd never ridden a bicycle before, but miraculously, he just started riding it down the hill. Out at the well, pumping her a drink of water, was Wilda Mae Wolfe. Clarence saw her and started heading right toward her. He didn't mean to, but he rammed the front wheel of my new bicycle right between her legs, and he just lapped her around a tree about fifteen feet from the well. You never heard a dying calf squall like Wilda Mae Wolfe did. Our teacher, Leo Pigg, got a big switch and wore it out on Clarence. During those days, teachers were allowed to physically punish their students, and frequently did.

"I have told this story probably fifty times at various churches during revival meetings. My wife, Betty, says, 'Someday you're going to tell that story, and Wilda Mae is going to be in the congregation.' And I say, 'Well, if she is, I'll just say, Wilda Mae, it's the truth, and you know it is the truth.' "

This quick wit and ability to use humor not only made Swad an effective communicator; it drew young men to him. He served as a mentor and model to some of the outstanding pastors who came out of south Missouri, including his own son, Dr. John Swadley. Several of the mega-church pastors I interviewed gave Paul Swadley credit for their calling to ministry and their development as effective leaders.

Ozarks humor is found in everyday things. Life on the farm is rich in funny stories and jokes. The church, the preacher, the deacon and the child in the pew supply many opportunities for humor. Interesting characters who live in the area provide stories that amuse, sometimes true stories, sometimes not so true.

Story Humor

Much of Ozarks humor is not the typical joke with a setup and a punch line. It is more in the nature of storytelling. The story may be long and involved, and the humor may be sprinkled through it, as well as some unexpected twist at the end.

In his book, *Ozarks Mountain Humor,* W. K. McNeil relates one of these folk tales that probably was repeated throughout communities all over the Ozarks. He records the story in the grammar and syntax of an early Ozarker. "There's a woman they thought she's dead and they started to the graveyard with her, they started into the gate with her, and the wagon wheel hit a post, and jarred the wagon, and she came to. She lived a long time after that and she died and they started back through the gate with her, and the old man said to be careful and don't hit the post again." [38]

One source of humor was found in drawing the contrast between the way of life of the typical Ozarker and that of the "city slicker." The comparison with city slickers sometimes took the form of the self-effacing acknowledgement that rural Ozarkers were much later getting indoor plumbing than their urban counterparts. In other cases, the humor was clearly intended to show that the Ozarker was more "savvy" than the city slicker.

In his joke book called, *Banjophil's Really Good Joke Book,* entertainer and humorist Phil Greer relates one of hundreds of stories about outhouses. Greer says, "My bathroom caught fire this morning. I was lucky, though, because they got it put out before it spread to the house." [39]

McNeil tells one such story that pits the city slicker against the common sense rural wisdom of the hillbilly. "Two city fellows were lost in the woods one day and they came upon an old hillbilly and asked him where they were, but the hillbilly said, 'I don't know.' Then they asked him how to get back to town, but the hillbilly said, 'I don't know.' Everything they asked the hillbilly he would always say he didn't know. Finally, one of the city boys said, 'Say, mister, you just don't know anything, do you?' And the old hillbilly answered, 'Maybe not, but I ain't lost.'" [40]

Humor about Church

Because religion was so much a part of life for our Ozarks ancestors, much of their humor came from church. Sometimes those stories were at the expense of the preacher. The preacher was generally a respected leader of the community, but he was also considered "other than a regular guy." Folks would clean up their language if a preacher was present, but they would also kid him good-naturedly about the length or quality of his sermons or his preference for fried chicken at mealtime.

Greer writes, "After the church service a little boy told the pastor, 'When I grow up, I'm going to give you some money.' 'Well, thank you,' the pastor replied, 'but why?' 'Because my daddy says you're one of the poorest preachers we've ever had.'" [41]

Children are much valued in the context of church life in the Ozarks. Many stories are told about things children said at church and at home related to God, religion, heaven, hell and other things considered sacred. One such story is, "A little boy opened the big family Bible. He was fascinated as he fingered through the old pages. Suddenly, something fell out of the Bible. He picked up the object and looked at it. What he saw was an old leaf that had been pressed in between the pages. 'Mama, look what I found,' the boy called out. 'What have you got there, dear?' With astonishment in the young boy's voice, he answered, 'I think it's Adam's underwear!'" [42]

Good-Natured Humor

Most of the humor of the Ozarks is self-effacing and not intended to be hurtful to anyone. The person telling the story is frequently the "butt of the joke." Even when the joke is on someone else it is usually not intended to be denigrating or malicious. The jokes may not always be "politically correct," but they are seldom intended to be mean.

Three of those whom I interviewed served as college presidents in Missouri, Dr. Arthur Mallory (Southwest Missouri State University), Dr. Thomas S. Field (William Jewell College and Missouri Baptist University), and Dr. Harlan Spurgeon (Southwest Baptist University). Even in that sophisticated world of academia, the Ozarks leader knows the value of humor and has a ready supply of funny stories. The same stories that entertained and amused whittlers sitting around the potbelly stove at the General Store, bring a chuckle at the after-dinner speech or the commencement ceremony.

Chapter Ten – Leadership Quality: Faith

"We believe..."

"For I know the plans I have for you, says the Lord. They are plans for good and not for evil, to give you a future and a hope." Jer. 29:11 (TLB)

The true leader believes some things. He or she has a core of conviction from which life is lived and leadership arises. One way of expressing this is to say that the leader is a "self-differentiated personality." If the person who aspires to leadership does not distinguish him or herself from the masses, there is no opportunity to step forward and lead. Without being arrogant or demeaning others, the leader says, "This I believe," or "Here I stand."

For many Ozarkers, that core of conviction is at least partially developed as religious faith. The highly-churched culture guides persons toward being self-aware and self-reflective through the experience of faith and the examination of their faith tradition. This does not mean that Ozarkers necessarily adopt the dominant religion or join the church of their parents, but it means that the processing of faith gives the opportunity to form basic beliefs.

A Religious Heritage

The Ozarks is located in an area of the country which some have called, "the buckle of the Bible belt." One cannot begin to understand the culture of the Ozarks without giving attention to the religion that was formational to the culture. While the place of the church and religious faith in society is not as prominent today as it once was, it is a vital part of the history and anthropology of the Ozarks.

The middle part of the 20th century was characterized by a religious fervor that involved revival meetings, brush arbor services, and "the sawdust trail" as the most common expression of religion. The sawdust trail referred to the sawdust used to create an aisle on the ground under a tent or brush arbor. Persons wishing to profess their faith were urged to "walk the aisle."

Most evangelical churches had a spring revival meeting and a fall revival meeting, working around the schedules of planting and harvesting of crops. In the summer, Vacation Bible School brought a week or two of organized church-based education for the children and a break from summer chores on the farm.

These experiences gave many Ozarks children not only a deeper education about faith and the Bible, but their first opportunities to lead. Children were encouraged to participate in the classes and sometimes lead portions of the classes and services. There were opportunities to sing, speak and share testimonies. Many Ozarks leaders trace their earliest leadership training and opportunities to their church experience.

Historian and educator Brooks Blevins notes, "From the early days of Ozark settlement, religion and churches played an integral role in migration patterns and community development. Faith was a valued tool of the frontier; it served as a commission to 'work till Jesus comes' and as a balm in times of hardship and distress. The rural church was as integral to Ozark life as was the smokehouse, the corn row, and the cold-water spring." [43]

Jim Webb, in *Born Fighting*, traces that religious history back to its European origins. He notes that Scottish Presbyterians migrating through Ireland and then to the New World became the "forerunners of the fundamentalist Christian movement in the United States." [44]

Protestants and Catholics

This preference for a Protestant approach to faith found fertile soil in the Appalachians, and the people spread that faith as they migrated west to the Ozarks and to the South. It came to be expressed under many denominational names: Assembly of God, Baptist, Church of Christ, Disciples of Christ, Methodist, Nazarene, Pentecostal, Presbyterian, and many others. These churches are scattered across the Ozarks in cities, towns, villages and the open country.

While the Protestant faith was predominant in Ozarks culture, there was a sizable representation of Catholicism in many communities. This difference in denominational perspective led to much kidding in many communities. Some was good-natured and some not so good-natured.

The humor directed toward priests and nuns was often biting and frequently off-color. One less offensive story about Catholics is: "One time a woman came in and asked a priest to have a funeral for her cat. 'That's ridiculous! Who ever heard of having a funeral for a cat?' the priest asked. She said, 'Father, you've got to. I've been everywhere, to the Baptist church, the Methodist church, and no one will take my money for holding the service.' The priest asked, 'How much were you willing to pay?' She said, 'Oh, five hundred dollars, I guess.' 'Hmm,' said the priest, 'that was a Catholic cat wasn't it?'" [45]

Bi-Vocational Preachers

The Ozarks has a history of circuit-riding preachers, that is, ministers who in addition to farming or being merchants, travelled from one community to another on horseback to preach in small churches. Their only pay from the ministry may have been an occasional chicken or some garden produce members of congregations could share with them. Some of these churches had services or saw a preacher only once or twice a month.

That tradition of the dedicated bi-vocational minister has continued to be a part of Ozarks church life. Hundreds of these God-called clergy largely made their livelihood in secular work and provided strong leadership for churches. Among the group of persons I interviewed for the book were several ministers who served in this way. They took on the challenge of holding a full-time secular job while concurrently leading a church.

Rev. Winston Burton had a long career as a public school administrator. He holds professional credentials both in education and in ministry. He is now retired as a high school principal but continues to work part-time as an educator with a local university. Through all of this, he has served as the pastor of First Baptist Church of Rogersville, Missouri.

Another of these effective bi-vocational ministers is Dr. Bob Marti. Bob holds a Doctor of Ministry degree and has served as a pastor throughout his working life, much of the time as a bi-vocational minister. He has worked as assistant athletic director for a university and as a businessman. Churches continue to benefit from the competent leadership and dedicated service of these ministers who carry on the tradition of the circuit-rider.

How Will You Be Remembered?

One of the ways in which the religious faith of my survey group emerged was in their responses to my questions about the music that they would want used at their funeral services and the epitaphs they would want engraved on their tombstones. Funeral music and the headstone phrases may be seen as the deceased's last opportunity to deliver a message to family and friends. Some of those surveyed were ministers, but most were lay persons.

Here are some of the responses to their preferences for funeral music:

"Because He Lives"
"The Servant Song"
"Be Strong in the Lord"
"Angel Band"
"Goodbye World, Goodbye"
"10,000 Reasons"
"I Can Only Imagine"
"Does Jesus Care?"
"Great Is Thy Faithfulness"
"How Firm a Foundation"
"Beulah Land"

These songs reflect both traditional and contemporary music choices. Some of the songs are in the southern gospel tradition. Many of them relate to heaven and to life beyond this earthly existence. Religion in the Ozarks, as in many other places of deep faith, offers hope and reassurance of God's care.

Tombstone epitaphs:

"He was a good and godly man"
"He served the Lord in his generation then fell asleep"
"Apply...forgiveness to the past, faith to the future, and yourself to the present"
"He walked with God"
"Saved by grace"
"He loved the Lord, and he loved his family"
"The key is to BE"
"He grew people and got them ready to grow"
"He was faithful"
"May All Who Come Behind Us Find us Faithful"

There is a humility expressed in these words. Ozarks leaders generally do not expect to be given great accolades for their professional accomplishments. They want to be remembered as "good" people in whatever way that word may be understood in their culture. They seek to serve God and to serve others by the way in which they live and die. They desire to honor the heritage into which they were born and to pass an even greater heritage on to those who follow them.

Robert L. Perry

Conclusion

Dear Child of the Ozarks,

Whether you were born and raised in the Ozarks or your parents or grandparents were, you can be proud of that heritage. If you came from elsewhere and adopted the Ozarks as your home, you can value and appreciate the unique qualities that helped create this place and its charm.

As you go other places and interact with other people, you need not feel inferior or intimidated by the strengths of their cultures. You can learn from those and value them, while affirming and claiming your own. If people dismiss you as a "hillbilly, hayseed, or redneck," know that they reveal more about their own lack of culture than any legitimate evaluation of yours.

Work hard, study well, be honest, lead with humility, laugh often, and tell your stories with passion. Compete to excel, but help others up as well. Remember where you came from and help those less fortunate.

See the world, learn other languages, have great adventures. But when you become weary and world-worn, find your way back to your roots. Walk through the woods on a carpet of leaves in the late fall. See the countryside glistening with a diamond-like covering of ice in the winter. Glory in the redbud and the dogwood as they color the hillsides in the spring. Go back to the swimming hole at the river on a hot summer day.

Listen for the voice of God in the breeze blowing through the treetops and the babble of the clear, spring-fed stream. See God's finger painting in the colors of the leaves in October. Smell the fresh-mown hay waiting to be baled. Wave at the farmer on his tractor, and sing with the congregation on Sunday morning.

 Live well and die contented,

Bob Perry

Robert L. Perry

Appendix

I want to introduce you to the outstanding people who were interviewed for this book. In the spirit of Ozarks informality, I decided to introduce them to you as I would if we were meeting face-to-face with a personal affirmation of how the person has impacted my life.

I want to introduce you to my friend, **Vernon Armitage**. I have known Vernon since we were students at Southwest Missouri State College (now Missouri State University). When he graduated and moved to Kansas City to go to seminary, he was serving as pastor of Mt. Zion Baptist Church, east of Ozark, MO. He recommended to the church that they call me to be his successor; and based on his affirmation, that good church became my first pastorate.

A couple of years later, I followed Vernon to the seminary in Kansas City. There we were not only fellow students, but we sang together in revival meetings and church services. Vernon played guitar and was the more competent musician, but I could sing harmony. As he finished his seminary degree, Vernon became pastor of Pleasant Valley Baptist Church in Liberty, MO. There he and his wife, Charlene, invested the next 41 years of their lives in leading that church from a weekly attendance of a hundred to an attendance of around 4,000 in weekly services.

After retirement from the ministry at Pleasant Valley, Vernon was still strong and vital. He became a staff pastor at Willow Creek Church in a suburb of Chicago, IL. There his ministry continued to grow and have a nation-wide impact. Vernon started at Chestnutridge, MO and continues to serve as a religious leader and trainer of leaders.

Let me introduce you to my friend, **Ann Ashcraft**. Ann grew up in Neosho, MO, where her father owned a furniture store and led music in various churches. She attended Oklahoma Baptist University, where she met and married a minister. Ann was taught to be resilient in spirit and optimistic by nature. She was affirmed as a leader by her parents, a very influential grandmother, school teachers, and pastors.

Ann and her husband moved around the country because of his various church positions. While he was a pastor in Florida, Ann used her training and expertise in early childhood education to assist Governor Lawton Chiles in developing some of the nation's first and best educational reforms. She also served as an educational specialist for churches, including River Road Church in Richmond, VA. Ann's self-confidence and strong work ethic have helped her lead in many settings as an educator and church woman.

Please meet my friend, **Hosea Bilyeu**. Hosea grew up as part of a large extended family on Bull Creek, near Chestnutridge, MO, the youngest of seven siblings. The Bilyeu family was heavily populated with musicians and preachers. Hosea started singing in church when he was six-years-old, comfortable being "up front." After several years as a high school math teacher, he attended seminary and became a fulltime pastor. I first met Hosea when he was a seminary student and I was back to the seminary working on a doctoral degree. I knew many of Hosea's relatives through college student religious and music groups.

Hosea led in the development of a great church, Ridgecrest Baptist Church, in Springfield, MO. He is a voracious reader and constant learner. Hosea has a deep and genuine identity with his Ozarks roots, and he also has an inquisitive mind and a creative spirit. He is as comfortable as a community leader and mentor to other ministers as he is preaching, playing his guitar and singing gospel music. Hosea, his wife Debbie, and their children sing together as The Bilyeu Family, and they plan to expand this and other ministries after his retirement as pastor at Ridgecrest.

My next friend (in alphabetical order) is **Winston Burton**. Winston and I met during college years through our involvement in the Baptist Student Union. We were both preparing for ministry, though we took different paths to that end. Winston continued his education and career development as a school teacher and administrator, while serving churches as a bi-vocational pastor.

Winston taught and did administrative work in the Springfield Public Schools and served as the pastor of First Baptist Church of Rogersville, MO for 38 years. That church has grown and expanded substantially and could easily have afforded to pay Winston for fulltime service. But by choice and calling, he continued his career as an educator while serving the church evenings and weekends. This led him to develop skills in delegating work to other part-time staff and volunteers. Winston believes that his approach to church encourages the laity to assume more responsibility and develop greater leadership ability.

Please meet my friend **Nolan Carrier**. He grew up on a farm near Lockwood, MO. Nolan is a great story teller and a natural extrovert and adventurer. His lifestyle creates stories (some of them almost unbelievable), and he is very skilled at telling stories. Nolan easily engages total strangers in conversations, and his genuine interest in their lives causes them to often share very personal and meaningful aspects of their lives with him.

Nolan felt called to be a minister at the age of fourteen. After attending college and seminary, he served as pastor of churches in Windsor, Ava and Springfield, MO. In 2012 he retired (briefly) as pastor of Southgate Baptist Church, but within a short time he became an interim pastor at Marionville, MO. Later he accepted a more permanent position as a bi-vocational pastor at Walnut Grove, MO.

Nolan is an avid St. Louis Cardinals fan, bicycle rider and tennis player. He has touched people throughout the Ozarks in deep and meaningful ways. For me personally, his friendship, genuineness, good humor and optimistic spirit are great gifts.

I would like for you to meet my friend **Bob Dale.** I first learned of Dr. Robert Dale when his book *To Dream Again* was required reading for one of my seminary classes. At that time Bob was working as a writer, editor and consultant with the Baptist Sunday School Board. He later became a seminary professor. When I moved to Virginia as a denominational executive in 1988, I found that Bob was the Associate Executive Director for the Baptist General Association of Virginia and the Director of the Center for Creative Church Leadership in Richmond, VA.

After we became personal friends we began to discover our common Ozarks heritage. Bob grew up near Neosho, MO, just 50 miles from my hometown of Verona. We shared a farming background, small church heritage of the Ozarks and many common values and interests. My wife and I had the opportunity to work with Bob for about 15 years through his leadership center, and he became a great friend and mentor to us both.

Bob is a life-long learner, an avid reader, and a prolific writer of books. He is widely published and has been a great encourager to me and many others who have an interest in writing. In the years that I have known Bob he has studied and practiced master gardening, stained glass art, glass "slumping" (google it), and other hobbies. His influence in the lives of younger leaders is greater than any person I know.

Now let me introduce my friend, **Thomas Field**. Dr. Field was my pastor during college where he served the great First Baptist Church in Springfield, MO. When I moved from the farm to "the big city" for college, I was in awe of the beauty and grandeur of this church and of its distinguished and powerful preacher. Dr. Field was an orator of broad vocabulary and an artist with words. He became a model of Christian faith and service for me and many other young men.

I had the great privilege of reconnecting with Dr. Field when I returned to Missouri in 2003. We often met for lunch and had great conversations. In 2005 he turned 90 years of age, and he was still serving as a development consultant for Missouri Baptist University in St. Louis, MO. He previously served as president of both William Jewell College at Liberty, MO and MBU in St. Louis.

One of the things I most admired about Dr. Field was his ability to adapt to various cultures and succeed as a leader in each. He grew up in the Chicago area, but he served churches in New York City, Georgia, Louisiana, and Missouri. He lived the most years in the Ozarks and made it his adopted home. In May of 2009, he died at the age of 93 and went to his heavenly reward. And I am sure that reward is great.

Meet my friend, **Mike Haynes.** Dr. Michael Haynes is the Director of Missions (regional church executive) for Greene County Baptist Association in Springfield, MO. I have known Mike since our seminary days. He grew up in northeast Oklahoma, if not officially a part of the Ozarks, a very similar culture and just a few miles from southwest Missouri and northwest Arkansas. Mike adopted the Ozarks as his home and is recognized as a significant leader in both the church environment and the broader community.

Having been a pastor for many years, Mike now serves as a "pastor to pastors." He is held in great esteem by pastors of churches large and small, rural and urban, throughout southwest Missouri. In addition to his professional leadership, Mike is a great family man and a model for faithful family life. Mike's philosophy of leadership is expressed in his book *The Key is to Be,* and his own example shows that being a faithful follower of Christ comes before the doing of the things Christians should do.

I am honored to introduce you to my friend, **Waylen Jobe**. I met Brigadier General Waylen Jobe when I became interim pastor of the church he attends in Willard, MO. He and his wife, Faith, have lived for many years at Willard. Originally born in Paragould, Arkansas, Waylen began his service in the Army in 1954. He was commissioned as an officer in 1959, making his way through the ranks to be made a general in 1984. He gave a total of 32 years to the uniformed service of his country.

The General completed training schools as an infantry officer, heavy mortar combat, transportation officer, fixed wing aviation, rotary wing aviation among other specialized training. During the years of the Vietnam Conflict he was the commander of a National Guard helicopter base in Springfield, Missouri. He was responsible for the repair of damaged helicopters flown in from Vietnam. At the time of his retirement he was the Brigade Commander of the 35th Engineer Brigade of the Missouri National Guard, Jefferson Barracks, St. Louis, MO.

General Jobe enjoys retirement these days as he and Faith spend time with children, grandchildren and great grandchildren. He came to faith in Christ after he married Faith, due to her influence and that of her very devout parents. They are active in their church, and Waylen rides his golf cart from his house to the nearby course to play golf when the weather permits.

Please meet my friend **Arthur Mallory**. I first met Arthur when he came to be the youngest president in the history of Southwest Missouri State College (now Missouri State University) when I was a sophomore. While he was president of the college, he taught the college men's Sunday School class I attended at First Baptist Church in Springfield. Arthur grew up at Buffalo, Missouri, where his father was the highly respected Superintendent of Schools. He earned his undergraduate degree at SMS.

After service in the U. S. Army and being stationed in Munich, Germany, Arthur returned to Missouri and completed his Ph. D. at the University of Missouri. Following his years as the president of SMS, Arthur was named as the State Commissioner of Education for Missouri. In that role he led the state to establish the first special education program provided in public schools.

Arthur served in many roles within his church and in the larger denomination at the state and national levels. He says that his model for leadership is the Old Testament prophet Nehemiah. From that prophet he learned to focus on the task at hand, involve other people in getting the job done, be generous in giving credit to those who do the work, and pray for guidance from God.

Meet my friend and extended family member, **Bob Marti**. Dr. Marti is married to my first cousin, Barbara. He grew up on a farm near Stotts City, Missouri, and attended high school at Mount Vernon, Missouri. Bob and his older brother, Richard, were very active in sports, and Bob has served for many years as an official for Missouri high school basketball and football.

Bob served as pastor of many Missouri churches, both large and small. For a number of years he has been a bi-vocational pastor while making a living as the Assistant Athletic Director for Southwest Baptist University and a businessman. At the time of this writing he is the pastor of Center Baptist Church at Ash Grove, MO.

Bob enjoyed life on the farm and has fond memories of those years. He went to a one-room school during his elementary school years. His family did not have an indoor bathroom when he was young. He learned the value of hard work, and he wanted to be a veterinarian when he was a boy. He felt called to be a minister at the age of 14, and that decision set the course for the rest of his life.

May I introduce you to my friend, **Russell Newport**? Russell grew up at Buffalo, Missouri where his father owned and operated a grocery store and a hardware store. Russell's mother was musical; she saw her son's talent. She started his voice lessons when he was 14 years-of-age.

After his graduation from William Jewell College at Liberty, Missouri, Russell joined the Navy in 1943. He was stationed on a destroyer with a home port at San Francisco, California. He received permission and encouragement from his ship's commander to begin a band on the ship, and he was able to sing with church choirs in San Francisco when off duty. After his discharge from the Navy, Russell utilized the GI Bill to pursue an MBA degree at Harvard University. While there, he studied voice at the New England Conservatory of Music.

Russell developed and managed a chain of stores scattered throughout southwest Missouri – eleven stores in all. While managing these and other businesses, he served as the minister of music at First Baptist Church of Springfield from 1949 till 1964. He also taught business courses at Southwest Missouri State. Russell's career as an accomplished tenor took him across the country and literally around the world. For about 30 years he spent a large portion of his time touring and recording. His powerful tenor voice continues to bless those who hear him at the age of 93.

The youngest of all the persons I interviewed for the book is my friend **Ryan Palmer**. Ryan grew up at Joplin, Missouri, and though he didn't live on a farm, his life was very involved with "bucking hay bales" in the summers, taking care of horses and shoveling manure. Ryan is the pastor of a large church in Springfield, Missouri, and he provides pastoral care for a number of members of my extended family.

Ryan was greatly influenced by his mother and father, especially with regard to his faith. His dad taught him to respect his mother and all women, to be loyal to the church, and to be resilient in the face of obstacles in life. He had a pastor and a youth minister who were significant influences during his teenage years. He also learned from the several coaches who were important leaders of his development in high school. Ryan recently completed his doctor of ministry degree, and he provides stable and progressive leadership for South Haven Baptist Church.

Please meet my friend **Patti Penny**. Patti is beautiful and smart. She grew up on a farm near Seymour, Missouri. One of the common experiences Patti and I remember from the farm was riding the hay mower. Poor farmers converted old horse-drawn mowers to be pulled by a tractor. To make that system work, someone had to drive the tractor while a second person (usually a kid) rode the mower to raise and lower the tines with a foot pedal. From these humble beginnings Patti became a topnotch entrepreneur – one of the outstanding female CEOs in southwest Missouri.

After beginning work as a secretary, she became a personnel specialist with a couple of large companies in Springfield. In 1988 she started her own business called Penmac Staffing Services, Inc. Penmac grew to be a multi-state company providing personnel training and placement services to many organizations. She is a natural leader and organizer. Patti is a deacon in her church and a philanthropist in her community. She is not afraid to lead, but she is happy to do much of her work behind the scenes.

This tall distinguished gentleman is my friend, **Bill Rowe**. Bill is the retired Athletic Director for Missouri State University. He grew up near Marionville, Missouri, and his family attended Buck Prairie Baptist Church, which his grandfather helped to found. Bill's dad farmed and worked at the numerous apple and peach orchards around Marionville. Bill milked cows and made hay and did other tasks on the farm, but he was also motivated to get off the farm.

Bill's great love in junior high and high school was baseball. He had great mentors for his baseball development, like Jeff Viles and Jerry Hillhouse. Men like these were a positive influence for his growth as a ball player and as a man. After high school Bill played baseball at Southwest Missouri State College where he had a great career. Later he became the baseball coach, and eventually the college named him as Athletic Director. A part of Bill's motivation in that role was to try to do for other young people what was done for him. He quotes another coach, Norm Stewart, who said, "When you see a turtle on top of a fence post, one thing you know for sure is that it didn't get there by itself."

Bill is a consistent and conscientious churchman. He is loved and appreciated by those who have been his pastors over the years, including Paul Swadley and Ryan Palmer (other members of my survey group). What began as a journey of faith when Bill was saved and baptized in a creek at the age of eight has brought him through good times and bad.

Here is my friend **Harlan Spurgeon**. Harlan has the heart of a missionary and the skills of a CEO. He grew up in Bolivar, Missouri, where his dad was a mail carrier. After attending Southwest Baptist College (now University) and William Jewell College, Harlan pursued his calling as a minister by attending The Southern Baptist Theological Seminary in Louisville, Kentucky. He later completed a doctoral degree.

Harlan and his wife Joann served as missionaries to Taiwan for fifteen years. Returning to the U. S. following that service he became the pastor of his home church, First Baptist of Bolivar. Later, Harlan was asked to become the president of Southwest Baptist College. After four years there, Dr. Keith Parks offered him the position of Vice President for Personnel of the Foreign Mission Board of the Southern Baptist Convention. Later, he became the associate to Dr. Parks in the leadership of the global missions efforts of the Cooperative Baptist Fellowship.

Since retiring, Harlan served two terms as President of the Baptist General Convention of Missouri (a.k.a. Churchnet) and interim pastor of six churches. He and Joann are involved in leadership in their church and are active in volunteerism.

I want to introduce you to my friend **Paul Swadley**. Paul is the son of an Ozarks preacher, Rev. L. V. Swadley, and his wife Elizabeth is the daughter of a preacher, Rev. John Youngblood. Paul says that the advice he got from his dad was, "Preach the Word; love the people." His first pastorate was a quarter-time church where he was paid $15.00 a week to show up and preach twice a month. From that humble beginning he went on to complete his seminary training, commuting to Kansas City, and served other churches around south Missouri. He spent 25 years as pastor of South Haven Church in Springfield.

Swad's ministry was built on loving people. His good humor and positive spirit attracted young and old. I don't know of a pastor who has encouraged and mentored more younger men in ministry. Swad says, "I love working with those who want to grow."

Finally, let me introduce you to my friend, **Chuck Williams**. Chuck grew up at Lewisburg, Missouri, and attended high school at Buffalo, Missouri, graduating as valedictorian. His high school basketball team won two state championships. He then played for Southwest Missouri State where his teams won three conference titles and finished second in NCAA Division II in 1969. While completing his Ph. D. in Biomechanics at the University of Indiana, he served on the coaching staff of Bobby Knight.

Chuck continued his coaching career serving as an assistant coach at SMS. In 1977 he became the head coach of the Missouri Southern University Lions. Under his leadership the Lions won two conference championships and went to seven NAIA District Tournaments. By the time he left in 1989, the Lions had amassed 182 wins with Chuck as their coach.

Chuck became a Christian during his senior year of high school. He has maintained a strong and vital faith ever since. One of the great strengths he brings to leadership roles, whether at church or in sports, is the ability to create teamwork. Chuck says, "I try to teach a person to give up himself for the sake of the team. I teach them to show respect for themselves and each other. I nip in the bud anything that destroys teamship."

About the author:

Bob Perry grew up on a farm west of Verona, Missouri. He became a Baptist minister and served as a pastor for 15 years, later becoming the executive director of associations of churches in Missouri and Virginia. He served as an international missionary in Mexico for seven years. In 2014 he will celebrate 50 years as a minister.

He pursued education as a way to "escape" the hard life of the farm, but has come to appreciate and treasure the experiences of growing up on an Ozarks farm. After traveling the world and living in huge urban centers, he returned to the Ozarks in 2003. Bob and his wife, Marilyn, live on eight acres a few miles west of Springfield, Missouri. He serves as a church consultant and provides ongoing ministry through Churchnet (the Baptist General Convention of Missouri) and the Greene County Baptist Association.

Dr. Robert L. Perry graduated as valedictorian at Verona High School. After earning a Bachelor of Science in Education degree from Missouri State University, he completed Master of Divinity and Doctor of Ministry degrees at Midwestern Seminary. This is the seventh book of which he has been author or co-author. His website is:
www.organizationalhealth.org

Bibliography

Blevins, Brooks. *Hill Folks: A History of Arkansas Ozarkers and Their Image.* Chapel Hill: University of North Carolina Press, 2002.

Blevins, Brooks. Interview in his office at Missouri State University on April 3, 2013.

Carter, Jimmy. *An Hour Before Daylight: Memories of a Rural Boyhood.* New York, NY: Simon and Schuster, 2001.

Greer, Phil. *Banjophil's Really Good Joke Book.* Cassville, MO: Helium Brothers Publishing, 2005.

Hartman, Mary and Elmo Ingenthron. *Bald Knobbers: Vigilantes on the Ozarks Frontier.* Gretna, LA: Pelican Publishing Co., 1988.

McCrumb, Sharyn. *The Songcatcher.* New York, NY: Penguin Putnam, Inc., 2001.

McNeil, W. K. *Ozark Country.* Jackson, MS: University of Mississippi Press, 1995.

McNeil, W. K. *Ozarks Mountain Humor.* Little Rock, AR: August House, Inc., 1989.

Rafferty, Milton D. *The Ozarks Land and Life.* Fayetteville, AR: The University of Arkansas Press, 2001.

Remini, Robert V. *The Life of Andrew Jackson.* New York, NY: Harper & Row, 1988.

Webb, Jim. *Born Fighting.* New York, NY: Broadway Books, 2004.

Wilson, Charles Morrow. *The Bodacious Ozarks: True Tales of the Backhills.* Gretna, LA: Gretna Publishing Co., 2002.

Wikipedia: http://en.wikipedia.org/wiki/Agrarianism

Wikipedia: http://en.wikipedia.org/wiki/Baldknobbers

Wikipedia: http://en.wikipedia.org/wiki/Pennsylvania_Dutch

ENDNOTES:

[1] Rafferty, *The Ozarks Land and Life,* 5.
[2] Blevins, Interview on 4-3-2013.
[3] Ibid.
[4] Ibid.
[5] McNeil, *Ozark Country,* 1.
[6] Rafferty, *The Ozarks Land and Life,* 2.
[7] McNeil, *Ozark Country,* 5-7.
[8] Wilson, *The Bodacious Ozarks,* 2.
[9] Ibid., 3.
[10] McNeil, *Ozark Country,* 9-16.
[11] Webb, *Born Fighting,* 38.
[12] Ibid., 133.
[13] Carter, *An Hour Before Daylight,* 18.
[14] Wikipedia, Agrarianism.
[15] Wikipedia, Pennsylvania Dutch.
[16] Blevins, *Hill Folks,* 133.
[17] Ibid., 272.
[18] McNeil, *Ozark Country,* 59.
[19] Ibid., 59.
[20] Ibid., 78.
[21] Ibid., 288.
[22] Ibid., 291-2.
[23] Ibid., 294.
[24] Ibid., 298.
[25] Webb, *Born Fighting,* 161.
[26] Carter, *An Hour Before Daylight,* 18.
[27] Webb, 343.
[28] Webb, *Born Fighting,* 3.
[29] Carter, *An Hour Before Daylight,* 18.
[30] McNeil, *Ozark Country,* 70-1.
[31] Wilson, *The Bodacious Ozarks,* 91.
[32] Ibid., 143-5.
[33] McNeil, *Ozarks Mountain Humor,* 59-60.
[34] Ibid., 54.
[35] Webb, *Born Fighting,* 256-9.
[36] McCrumb, *The Songcatcher,* 1-11.
[37] McNeil, *Ozark Country,* 70.
[38] McNeil, *Ozarks Mountain Humor,* 77.
[39] Greer, *Banjophil's Really Good Joke Book,* 28.

[40] McNeil, *Ozarks Mountain Humor,* 107.
[41] Greer, *Banjophil's,* 3.
[42] Ibid., 5.
[43] Blevins, *Hill Folks,* 51.
[44] Webb, *Born Fighting,* 99.
[45] McNeil, *Ozarks Mountain Humor,* 127-8.

Other Books by Bob Perry:

Find A Niche And Scratch It - Marketing Your Congregation. Jesus was uniquely adept in the art of "reading" people. He fit his approach to the precise needs and interests of the person with whom he was dealing, and he spoke the cultural language of that individual. In this book, Robert Perry takes what Jesus and others have done intuitively—niche marketing—and provides a system for applying those principles in everyday practice. Convinced that congregations can learn from the wisdom of secular disciplines and apply that wisdom to congregational life, without damaging the integrity of the Christian faith, Perry offers a detailed process for using sound marketing principles to identify a congregation's strengths and the needs of its community, and to develop strategies for effective ministry. $15.00

Manual for Values-based Tactical Planning is a complete leader's guide for this totally new approach to strategic planning. It is right-brain, visionary and effective. The planning process includes the identification of the core values of the group, the writing of a mission statement and the development of a plan for an effective future. Written by Bob Perry, Ray Spears, and Stephen Welch. $25.00

Pass the Power, Please! is the easy-to-read story of how one pastor and a group of lay leaders learned to understand and work with the power structures of the church. The book delineates the ways in which the formal power systems of the church interact with the informal. Various tools for identifying and working with power persons are included, as well as ideas appropriately empowering the laity in a church. $10.

FuturOpting: How Churches Can Do Multiple-scenario Planning applies the insights and methodologies of scenario planning to local church applications. This planning approach is the most visionary and provides the longest-term plan of any way of strategizing. Futuropting allows a church to take responsibility for its future, and it reduces the level of systemic anxiety. $7.00

Congregational Wellness: Help for Broken Churches is a 140-page paperback with a family systems approach to understanding how churches experience health and dysfunction. The book contains case studies of many congregations that illustrate the ways in which congregational health may be diagnosed, and it suggests practical ways for improving the health of a church. $10.00

To order any of these email: bob@organizationalhealth.org

Phone: 417-742-0991